PLANNING FOR EFFECTIVE TECHNICAL TRAINING

A Guide for Instructors and Trainers

D1709786

PLANNING FOR EFFECTIVE TECHNICAL TRAINING

A Guide for Instructors and Trainers

Jerrold E. Kemp and George W. Cochern

Emeritus Professors
San Jose State University

Educational Technology Publications
Englewood Cliffs, New Jersey 07632

Library of Congress Cataloging-in-Publication Data

Kemp, Jerrold E.
    Planning for effective technical training : a guide for
instructors and trainers / Jerrold E. Kemp, George W. Cochern.
        p. cm.
    Includes bibliographical references and index.
    ISBN 0-87778-267-9
    1. Teaching. 2. Teaching--Aids and devices. 3. Technical
education. 4. Vocational education. I. Cochern, George W.
II. Title.
LB1025.3.K46 1994
371.'02--dc20   93-28872
                                                        CIP

Printed in the United States of America.

Library of Congress Catalog Card Number:
93-28872.

International Standard Book Number:
0-87778-267-9.

First Printing: January, 1994.

THE AUTHORS

Jerrold E. Kemp has an Ed. D. degree in Instructional Technology from Indiana University. For 30 years he was a Professor of Instructional Technology and Coordinator of Instructional Development Services at San Jose State University, California.

He is author of two books — **The Instructional Design Process** and **Planning, Producing, and Using Instructional Media**. Contributions have been made to other textbooks and journals in the media field.

Dr. Kemp serves as a consultant and conducts workshops for trainers in business and industry on instructional planning and the development of instructional media.

George W. Cochern holds a Ph.D. in Educational Media from Syracuse University. He was a Professor of Instructional Technology at San Jose State University for 36 years.

As co-author, or illustrator/photographer, he contributed to a number of publications including four books relating to media and training. He is currently involved in conducting workshops on the development of training presentations and instructor-presentation skills.

ACKNOWLEDGMENTS

A number of qualified persons, representing the variety of audiences for this book, were asked to review the manuscript. The authors express their thanks for the thoughtful comments and useful suggestions received from the following:

Don Betando
    Professor, Division of Technology
    San Jose State University
    San Jose, California

Fred Estes
    Corporate Training and Economic Development
    Mission College
    Santa Clara, California

Tom Campbell
    Instructor, SMT Numerical Control and Robotics
        and
Margo Davis
    Instructional Design Consultant
    Hewlett-Packard Company
    Palo Alto, California

Jim Sidow
    Manager, Training and Education
        and
Ilona Serrao
    Senior Course Designer
    VMX, Inc.
    San Jose, California

Dale Silva
    Senior Technical Trainer
    Sun Microsystems, Inc.
    Mountain View, California

Contents

Section C: PUTTING IT ALL TOGETHER

Introduction

HOW WILL THIS BOOK HELP YOU?

"Have you recently been assigned to conduct training?"
"How should you start?"
"What planning and preparation are necessary?"
Or ... "Are you now involved in training and you would like to do a better job of developing and delivering your training?"

Often a trainer feels that "to teach as one was taught" is the way to do it. But today's training situation is very different from what might have been successful in the past. These are some matters to recognize:

- Employees or students may be less well prepared to study and learn than formerly.
- We know more about how training can be structured so that learning can best happen.
- There are new resources to use to make learning more interesting and successful.

This book is designed for persons who have technical competencies but limited knowledge or experience in teaching. Very likely, you may be on your own to decide how to prepare for your teaching. These chapters will provide you with the information and procedures that can guide you in designing and delivering quality instruction.

We use the expressions **competency-based training** and **mastery learning** to describe the anticipated results for the approach to planning taken here. They apply to training programs that are systematically designed to qualify students for successful job performance.

Two Approaches to Training

There are two major approaches to training. You may use either one, or a combination of the two.

The first is the conventional **instructor-student, face-to-face** method. It is mainly classroom-based as the instructor presents information, demonstrates procedures and skills, and sets the pace for learning. The students or trainees take notes and may ask questions. Lab activities or other applications of the information learned follows the lecture session.

The other approach to training is more **student-centered**, requiring a greater degree of activity by students. It can give better attention to what is known about how people learn. For example, we recognize that individuals learn at different rates and in different ways. This means that instruction might be provided in a flexible way, allowing each student to progress individually while using appropriate resources, in order to meet objectives within a preset deadline.

As part of this new approach, other opportunities may need to be provided for small group or team activities as students share information and support each other while learning. This pattern of training, with the increasing availability of sophisticated, interactive resources, allows students to learn **faster** and **better**, while attaining higher levels of competency. Rather than primarily a lecturer, the instructor becomes more of a guide, coach, and evaluator to certify competence.

This book will provide the information necessary for designing and implementing technical training in both forms of instruction. Conventional teaching procedures, on-the-job training, and non-traditional methods with newer resources, all receive attention.

The following questions will be treated within the chapters of the book:

Design:
- **Why Must This Subject be Taught?**
- **What Am I Supposed to Teach?**
- **How Do I Write Objectives?**
- **Who Are My Students?**
- **How Can I Do the Teaching?**
- **What Resources Can I Use?**
- **How Do I Test Student Learning?**

Develop:
- **How Do I Prepare Various Types of Instructional Materials?**
- **How Do I Develop an Instructional Plan and a Lesson Plan?**
- **How Do I Develop a Flexible, Self-Instructional Plan and On-the-Job Training?**

Implement:
- **How Do I Carry-Out Classroom Instruction?**
- **How Do I Manage a Self-Paced Learning Program and On-the-Job Training?**

Evaluate:
- **How Do I Determine Training Results?**

Legal Liabilities in Training

Consider these situations:

"I wasn't told these chemicals could hurt me!"
"I didn't know that operation of this equipment could be dangerous!"
"I wasn't shown how to protect myself while carrying out this procedure!"
"I didn't understand what was explained about safe practices during training!"
"It became stressful when I wasn't able to do the job properly!"

Each situation could lead to a legal claim that training was inadequate by not including forseeable job hazards or safety instructions. The person designing the training, or the instructor, might be held liable for not developing or delivering competent training.

By using the information and applying the procedures presented in this book, you will be better prepared to develop, deliver, and evaluate successful training. Also, you should be aware of regulations and statutes that can impose significant training requirements on employers and institutions.

Check with the legal office in your organization concerning requirements under the following, as well as other legal precedents and regulations, so you can avoid legal pitfalls.

- Occupational Safety and Health Act (OSHA)
- Equal Employment Opportunity Commission (EECO)
- Americans with Disability Act (ADA)
- Environmental Resources Act (ERA)
- Toxic Substance Control Act (TSCA)

Design of the Book

The book is divided into three sections:

Section A. Planning for Training
Section B. Preparing Instructional Materials
Section C. Putting It All Together

Each chapter starts with a list of objectives that will be treated. Then, as each key point is presented, it is illustrated with one or more examples from a technical vocation. You should be able to relate the examples to applications in your own field. Due to space limitations, examples may not be fully developed, but sufficient information is included to illustrate the concept being presented.

Instructors frequently find the need to develop their own teaching materials. Therefore, a complete section of the book is devoted to general methods and specific techniques for preparing a range of audio and visual materials from simple chalkboard use to newer interactive media formats.

Procedures for evaluating student learning, by determining competency with specified objectives, receive careful consideration. Since increased recognition is being given to the need for establishing accountability of training program results, a final chapter describes how to determine the effectiveness, efficiency, and cost-benefits of a training course.

At the end of each chapter, you will find:

- a concise summary of the concepts presented;
- a review exercise to check your understanding of the content presented;
- a list of references for further information on chapter topics.

An **Epilogue** and a **Glossary** of definitions for important terms used in this book will be found following the last chapter.

Before starting to study the chapters, would you like to check your own knowledge and practices relating to instructional planning and teaching procedures? The next pages contain a **questionnaire** that can indicate your present level of understanding and your practices with respect to the many aspects of training to be covered. Check where you are now. You may be more knowledgeable than you believe you are!

WHAT DO YOU ALREADY KNOW ABOUT TRAINING PROCEDURES?

Before starting to use this book, check your present knowledge about training. Read each statement, then circle the number that represents your present position. Skip any items that you do not understand. (The number in (parenthesis) is the chapter treating the content.)

High   Low

5 4 3 2 1   1. I identify the justification for training (training needs) before starting to plan a training program. (1)

5 4 3 2 1   2. I list the topics for a subject I will teach. (2)

5 4 3 2 1   3. I carefully outline the content for a lesson plan. (2)

5 4 3 2 1   4. I detail a performance skill for a lesson plan. (2)

5 4 3 2 1   5. I develop a flowchart to describe a skill. (2)

5 4 3 2 1   6. I recognize the difference between a goal statement and objectives for students. (2,3)

5 4 3 2 1   7. I write objectives for each training session. (3)

5 4 3 2 1   8. My objectives relate to three categories of learning. (3)

5 4 3 2 1   9. Each objective consists of a carefully selected verb, content, and a performance standard. (3)

5 4 3 2 1   10. I find out the preparation that students have in basic skills. (4)

5 4 3 2 1   11. I find out what students already know about the subject to be studied. (4)

5 4 3 2 1   12. I attempt to give some recognition in my teaching to different learning styles of students. (4)

5 4 3 2 1   13. I recognize how adult learners differ from younger students. (4)

5 4 3 2 1   14. I recognize that there are training methods other than the classroom lecture.(5)

5 4 3 2 1   15. Lecturing is the method of instruction I mainly use for my teaching. (5)

5 4 3 2 1   16. I realize there are strong limitations to the lecture method. (5)

5 4 3 2 1   17. I use these small group learning methods in my class. (5)

5 4 3 2 1   a. Instructor/student discussion

5 4 3 2 1   b. Demonstrations

5 4 3 2 1   c. Laboratory activities

5 4 3 2 1   d. Simulations of real-life or problem situations

5 4 3 2 1   18. I assign students some type of individual, self-paced learning for studying certain content, including: (5)

5 4 3 2 1   a. Textbook or manual with worksheets for completion

5 4 3 2 1   b. Use of job aids

5 4 3 2 1   c. Computer-based training

5 4 3 2 1   d. Computer along with interactive media uses

5 4 3 2 1   19. I use various types of audiovisual media in my teaching. (6)

           20. I have experience with these media types: (6)

5 4 3 2 1   a. Chalkboard

5 4 3 2 1   b. Flipchart

5 4 3 2 1   c. Printed material on paper

5 4 3 2 1   d. Overhead transparency

5 4 3 2 1   e. Slide or Slide/tape program

5 4 3 2 1   f. Audio recording

5 4 3 2 1   g. Video recording

5 4 3 2 1   h. Computer technology

5 4 3 2 1   i. Interactive media

5 4 3 2 1   21. When I develop a test, the questions relate directly to the objectives for the topic. (7)

5 4 3 2 1   22. I apply standards of "competency-based" or "mastery learning" with my students. (7)

5 4 3 2 1   23. I use various types of objective and written-answer tests. (7)

5 4 3 2 1   24. When I test student skill performance, I use a checklist or a rating scale. (7)

5 4 3 2 1   25. I develop an instructional plan for the course I teach. (15)

5 4 3 2 1   26. I plan how each topic will be handled in my teaching. (15)

5 4 3 2 1   27. I develop a detailed lesson plan for each class session. (15)

5 4 3 2 1   28. I have developed self-instructional modules for individual student use. (16)

5 4 3 2 1   29. I have developed on-the-job training in my specialty. (16)

5 4 3 2 1   30. I pay attention to my appearance, speech, mannerisms, and other classroom presentation skills. (17)

5 4 3 2 1   31. I have analyzed my presentation skills by having at least one classroom session videotaped and reviewed. (17)

5 4 3 2 1   32. I have gathered data to show the effectiveness of my instruction. (18)

5 4 3 2 1   33. I use a questionnaire to gather student reactions to my teaching at the end of a course. (18)

5 4 3 2 1   34. I am available to my students after class sessions. (17)

5 4 3 2 1   35. I follow-up on my students after a course to determine how they are using the information and skills I taught. (18)

5 4 3 2 1   36. I use the results from a class for improvement the next time I teach the same subject. (18)

The above statements represent many of the main concepts presented in this book. All items may not be important in the training you conduct. How well did you do? Your replies indicate your present knowledge and experience.

Section A

PLANNING FOR TRAINING

As indicated in the Introduction, a series of questions can guide you in planning for carrying-out training. This section treats the seven essential elements of planning:

Chapter 1: Why Must This Subject be Taught?
Chapter 2: What Am I Supposed to Teach?
Chapter 3: How Do I Write Objectives?
Chapter 4: Who Are My Students?
Chapter 5: How Can I Do the Training?
Chapter 6: What Resources Can I Use?
Chapter 7: How Do I Test Student Learning?

INSTRUCTOR

NEEDS
CONTENT
OBJECTIVES
STUDENTS
METHODS
RESOURCES
TESTING

STUDENTS

You may already be familiar with many of these planning components. Some elements would be easy to treat, while others require more detailed efforts.

Although the planning stages will be examined in the order established by the set of questions, you may find it more comfortable or necessary to change the order, skip around, or move back and forth as you design your own training plans. Proceed in the way most comfortable or sensible to you. Some instructors like to start with an outline for a lesson plan or a training schedule (Chapter 15); then to fill-in details with the planning components presented in this section.

Your assignment may be for one topic like **Parallel Circuitry** to be taught during a single class session. Or, you may be responsible for a week of training, a set of self-instructional modules, or a course requiring a full semester that will include a number of topics in a subject area like **Refrigeration**. For each training program format, the same planning elements should be utilized.

The ultimate result of your planning will be the preparation of lesson plans or self-paced learning modules, and then carrying out the training. These matters will be covered in Section C.

Chapter 1

WHY MUST THIS SUBJECT BE TAUGHT?

In this chapter you will learn to:

> • **Recognize the importance of basing a training program on identified needs.**
> • **Indicate six general reasons for training.**
> • **Identify up to six specific justifications for revising a training program.**
> • **Relate four conditions or deficiencies that may need correction instead of initiating training.**
> • **Distinguish two categories, and the means within each one, for gathering data in support of a need.**
> • **Prepare a statement that justifies the need for training.**

Training Situation

If you are engaged in training within a company or similar organization, the answer to the chapter title question should be considered carefully. It should be based on the organization's goals. There are various reasons why training may take place:

- Level of performance on the job is below what is expected or required.
- Job requirements change, or new employees are hired.
- New equipment or new procedures must be learned.
- Safety needs are identified to reduce accident level.
- Training is mandated by regulations, industry, or union requirements.
- Professional development and upgrading knowledge or skills are important to employees.

Other, specific justifications to modify or revise a training program include:

- Course or training program is consistently rated LOW by students.
- Assigned training period or time required for training is longer than needed.
- Wish to change methods of instruction is expressed (often from conventional classroom lectures to more flexible, individual, self-paced learning with new resources).
- Evidence from the literature, recommendations from recognized experts, and reports from other training programs indicate an option for changes.
- Costs for an instructional program are too high.
- Teaching competency of instructor is rated low by students.
- Program changes are required for administrative reasons — budget limitations, personnel reductions, and so forth.

Academic Situation

If you are an instructor in a college or a vocational school, the answer to the above chapter title question seems to be obvious. A curriculum is established, courses are identified, and you are assigned teaching responsibilities. When decisions about course offerings were being made, consideration should have been given to identifying the **needs** relating to student competency in the craft or occupation.

This analysis of needs leads to the teaching of information and skills that comprise the curriculum and its courses. Periodically, each course should be examined and assessed as to how well it serves these needs.

Maybe Training Is NOT the Answer!

We have established the principle that when change or growth is required in knowledge, skills, or attitudes of employees or students, a training or educational program often becomes necessary. However, there are times when, on careful examination of the situation, the need cannot be clearly identified as one requiring an instructional answer. What is revealed, however subtle, may not be a training problem at all. Instead it may be one of the following:

- A personnel matter like low employee morale or poor supervision.
- A communication failure within the organization.
- A procedural matter like inadequate directions at worksite or inappropriate work standards.
- A poor facility or unsatisfactory equipment.
- Lack of suitable recognition for personnel like low pay, few benefits or rewards for individuals.
- External influences or situations beyond immediate or local control relating to policies, regulations, or governmental codes.

If you find evidence that any of these conditions is influencing either the request for a new instructional program or hindering the success of a program underway, then steps should be taken to overcome the existing problem by appropriate action **before** spending time on planning training. Unless such deficiencies are corrected, any program, old or newly established, could be destined to failure.

Gathering Data in Support of a Training Need

There are various ways to gather information, either to determine whether the need for a new instructional project does exist, or to support the modification of a present program. Needs analysis can be grouped into two categories — **internal analysis** procedures and **external analysis** procedures.

Internal Needs Analysis Procedures

Gather data from sources within the organization or institution as follows:

- Interview instructors and other staff members as to their observations and impressions about student competencies and attitudes.
- Talk with employees and former students concerning their own impressions and judgments as to the value and success of a

program, and also the needs they recognize which could be served through training.
- Observe personnel performing a job — take notes, complete checklists or even record video as evidence for analysis.
- Obtain factual information and opinions about job practices and needs from technicians, supervisors, and managers.
- Examine company records to determine production levels and product quality, personnel turnover rates, safety records, and other evidence as indicators for technical training needs.

Develop a survey form or prepare to conduct interviews by:

1. Drafting a list of questions.
2. Testing the questions with two or three representative individuals. Revise as necessary.
3. Distribute the survey or schedule the interviews.

Example of internal needs analysis:

Situation: A large company uses plastic film for packaging various products at its six plants. Much of the packaging operation is new, automated, with use of complex robotic equipment. It is reported that:
.. output quantity is less than planned
.. excess rejection of packaged products
.. excess waste of plastic material and product being packaged
.. frequent stop of production line for adjustments

Management personnel, supervisors, and technicians on the line were interviewed, using these questions:
1. Are the problems encountered due to equipment deficiencies or unsuitable material?
2. Is the production area efficient (lighting, noise, level, comfort, etc.)?
3. Do you know of other companies using this same equipment successfully? If successful, do they still have problems?
4. Have you contacted the equipment manufacturer about the problems?
5. Have the technicians been sufficiently trained and supervised to operate and maintain the equipment?
6. Are the technicians competent in their handling of equipment and materials?

Consensus answers:
1. No, the equipment is suitable.
2. No problems.
3. Do not know of any problems other companies might be having.
4. Yes. We have been assured the equipment is operating properly.
5. Technicians received an orientation when equipment was installed.
6. Most technicians feel that now, with full operation, they have questions and need specific help with settings, adjustments, loading procedures, and so forth.

External Needs Analysis Procedure

By visiting training programs at other organizations or institutions, and analyzing required knowledge, skills, and attitudes of individuals on the job, detailed external assessment can be made to supplement internal ones. The methods used may include:

- Interview training and/or educational personnel at other organizations, or managers, supervisors, and employees in job situations.
- Observe and analyze instructional programs at other institutions or on-the-job activities, and compare them with the requirements of local training and educational objectives.
- Distribute a questionnaire to survey present practices and recognized needs in the field.

Example of external needs analysis:
(Follow-up of above situation)

The equipment manufacturer was contacted. Also, representatives from two other companies, which use similar equipment to package different products, agreed to answer questions.

Manufacturer:
1. Had the equipment been properly installed and checked out?
2. How well qualified do you believe the technicians are to handle the operation?
3. What is your recommendation?

Answers:
1. Yes, we certified this.
2. We originally wanted to provide comprehensive training, but the company felt this was unnecessary.
3. Set up a training program for technicians. We will cooperate. Our equipment requires fairly sophisticated attention.

Other companies:
1. Have you had problems with your equipment when installed and first used?
2. Could there be a mismatch or other difficulty with the materials used with the equipment?
3. From your experience, what action do you recommend?

Answers:
1. It took time for our personnel to become proficient, even though our operation is smaller than that of this company.
2. Shouldn't be any problems. Equipment can be adjusted for various plastic films.
3. Set up a training program for their workers.

For job-oriented technical fields, useful information can be gathered from all sources, both internal and external. Particular attention should be given to external analysis sources because of the continual need to be competitive and up-to-date relative to required knowledge and skill competencies of employees.

For an academic-type program, use of internal analysis procedures is common. These should be supplemented with data collected from external sources, such as: similar courses at other institutions, practices in the field, and published reports.

Regardless of the methods by which information is obtained, the analysis requires reviewing, classifying, interpreting, and evaluating the data. Next judge what action would best serve the need or solve any problem found. This data-gathering process can be very brief and informal, or it can be extensive, requiring detailed summaries and statistical treatment. You must decide on the value, importance, and level of complexity for doing a needs analysis in your situation.

Training Needs Statement

Once a need for training is recognized and data are collected, a summary statement should be prepared. This will enable you to clearly answer these questions:

- What need or needs are identified?
- What evidence justifies each need?
- For which employees or job classification would training satisfy the need?
- How should training be organized?

Such a summary can apply to either a training or academic program. It would support a recommendation for a new or revised course, or even specific, limited training activity. With approval, you are ready to examine the instructional content and analyze the tasks to be performed.

Here is an example of a training needs statement for the packaging company illustration of needs assessment on pages 5, and 6.

> "Evidence from both the manufacturing company and other equipment-using companies supports the conclusion that the problems encountered are directly related to tasks required in operating and maintaining the production line equipment."
>
> **Recommendations:** Since technicians at the branch plants have received little specific training, a program should be organized to allow each person to gain full competency with the equipment and materials. It is recommended that a two-step training program be initiated immediately:
> 1. Have the manufacturer provide necessary training for a small group of supervisors or senior technicians (two per plant).
> 2. These qualified persons should then conduct classroom and on-the-job training for all technicians.

Summary

1. Reasons for training include: changes in job requirements; low performance levels; new equipment or new procedures to be learned; professional development for individuals; training required by regulations.

2. Periodically analyze an academic course to assess how well it serves the needs of the occupation.

3. Consider revising a training program when: learning or performance levels are below requirements; instructional costs are too high; training time is too long; you desire to change instructional methods; students are dissatisfied with present training; necessary changes are indicated from outside sources; administrative reasons require changes.

4. Needs not requiring instructional answers include: personnel matters, including lack of recognition; procedural matters; external influences.

5. Use internal and external analysis procedures to gather data.

6. Prepare a training needs statement to gain approval for start of training.

Review Exercise

1. Before starting to plan a training program or develop a vocational course, what should be done first?

2. Which of the following can justify training?
    a. Lighting levels are low in an assembly area and the number of assembled units has been decreasing.
    b. A new set of environmental regulations requires extensive changes in handling toxic wastes.
    c. A complex new procedure is to be introduced on the production line.
    d. Increasing numbers of safety violations are reported.
    e. It has been determined that many technicians have not been told to review recently approved requirements for international shipments.

3. What important analysis procedure(s) for gathering needs information is (are) **not** included in this list?
    a. Observing employees doing a job.
    b. Talking with former students about the value of training they received.
    c. Reviewing production, safety, and other records to determine whether levels are satisfactory.
    d. Distributing a survey form to supervisors for determining their views about job needs.

4. What are two possible **external analysis** procedures that can supplement internal procedures when establishing a training need?

5. For which reasons might you want to modify a training program for improvement?
    a. Training takes too much time.
    b. Recommendations for revisions are received from consultants.
    c. Someone informs you that a competitive company is revising their training programs.
    d. Management has decided there may be advantages to shifting a training program from one location to another one.
    e. Training costs need to be reduced.

6. What three major items should be included in a Training Needs statement?

Answers: 1. Determine if there is a <u>need</u> for the course or program.
        2. b,c,d, (a – facility matter, e – personnel communications matter).
        3. Examine company records concerning production levels, product quality, personnel turnover, safety records, etc.
        Talk with instructors about their beliefs as to the suitability of training courses being conducted.
        4. Interview appropriate personnel at other organizations.
        Observe training at other places.
        Distribute a questionnaire to survey practices in the field.
        5. a,b,e.

6. Needs that have been identified.
   Evidence that supports the need.
   Personnel or categories of employees who should be trained relative to the need.
   Recommended type of training.

References

Analyzing Performance Problems or "You Really Oughta Wanna." R. F. Mager and P. Pipe. Belmont, CA: Lake Publishing, 1984.

Figuring Things Out: A Trainer's Guide to Needs and Task Analysis. R. Zemke and T. Kramlinger. Reading, MA: Addison-Wesley, 1982.

Needs Assessment: Concept and Application. R. Kaufman and F. English. Englewood Cliffs, NJ: Educational Technology Publications, 1979.

Needs Assessment: A User's Guide. R. Kaufman and others. Englewood Cliffs, NJ: Educational Technology Publications, 1993.

"Selecting Needs Analysis Methods." J. Newstrom and J. Lilyquest. *Training and Development Journal,* 1979, *33*(10), 52-65.

Training Needs Assessment. A. Rossett. Englewood Cliffs, NJ: Educational Technology Publications, 1987.

"Strategic Needs Assessment." W. Rothwell. *Performance and Instruction,* 1984, *23*(5), 19-20.

Chapter 2

WHAT AM I SUPPOSED TO TEACH?

In this chapter, you will learn to:

- **State a goal for the subject.**
- **List topics for the subject.**
- **Select and outline subject content for the topic.**
- **Sequence or flowchart the procedure for skill development.**
- **Locate sources of information on a topic.**

State Goal for Subject

As an instructor, you are given a subject to teach. Begin your planning by deciding, in terms of the previously identified needs, what you should accomplish by teaching the subject. Write down this goal.

The goal, unlike an objective, is a broad statement of the general result required from training. It helps you determine the extent of the course. For example:

Subject: DIESEL ENGINES
Goal: To learn about the theory, operation, and maintenance of diesel engines

---

The important word used in stating a goal is a **verb**, like the following:

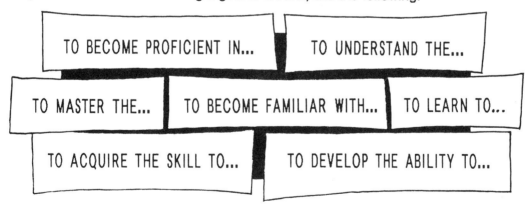

TO BECOME PROFICIENT IN...   TO UNDERSTAND THE...

TO MASTER THE...   TO BECOME FAMILIAR WITH...   TO LEARN TO...

TO ACQUIRE THE SKILL TO...   TO DEVELOP THE ABILITY TO...

In Chapter 3 you will be introduced to writing learning objectives. **Goals** and **objectives** *differ*. As stated, a goal is a broad statement of what is to be learned. Learning objectives are more specific. They indicate what a student will be able **to do** with the information and skills learned by the end of training.

List Topics for Subject

A subject consists of one or more topics. In terms of the stated goal, decide what topics to include. List them.

Here is an example of topics for a training subject:

Subject: INFORMATION PROCESSING

Goal: To understand computer hardware and software systems in use today

Topics: Computer as a System
Data Representation
Entering Data
Obtaining Information
Storing Data
Processing Data
Computer Operations

Once you have stated the goal and listed the topics for the subject, you are ready to proceed to the details of specifying content and skill procedures for each topic.

Select and Outline Subject Content

For any topic, the subject content may include both information and skill development. Start with the information and decide on the content for each topic. Outlining content is an essential part of the lesson plan you will develop in Chapter 15. The content outline may include information on three levels:

(1) facts, terms, and definitions
(2) descriptions, functions, and processes
(3) concepts, rules, principles, regulations, and legal codes

Here are examples of information on the three levels:

Subject: AUTOMOBILE ELECTRICAL SYSTEMS

(1) **Facts** — 12 volt battery required
    Negative ground used on most cars
  Terms — Ammeter, voltmeter, starter solenoid, fuse, sealed beam headlight
  Definitions — The **alternator** produces electrical power
    The **coil** takes a small amount of voltage from the alternator and multiplies it to higher voltage for firing spark plugs

(2) **Descriptions** — A blown fuse no longer has a continuous filament
    Colored coded wires connect battery to electrical accessories
  Functions — Ignition switch closes circuit to allow current to flow from battery to starter
    A feeler gauge checks gap in spark plug points
  Processes — Periodically clean and tighten battery cable connections
    If starter does not turn over, check battery cable connections and battery charge

---

(3) **Concepts** — Electronic ignition system, maintenance-free battery, cold cranking amps (CCA)
    Rules (principles) — A cold engine is harder to start than is a warmer engine
      The negative cable from battery is connected directly to metal car frame
    Regulations — Both headlights must be correctly aimed and function properly on low and high beams

Follow this procedure to select and organize information for a topic:

1. Write down the **major questions** about the topic the students should be able to answer as the result of instruction.
2. Review the questions, to be certain they are in a logical order.
3. Outline the information you will present to enable the student to answer each question.

While applying the above procedure, keep in mind the level of student knowledge and understanding you can expect at the start of training. (Explanations in Chapter 4 will help you to determine this.) Plan to lead students logically from simple information to be learned, to complex understandings, applications, and problem solving activities. See page 141 for further suggestions for organizing and sequencing subject content.

Here is an example of a subject content outline:

Topic: FIRE EXTINGUISHERS
Goal: To know how to select and use a fire extinguisher
Questions: 1. What are the kinds of extinguishers?
    2. What special features about extinguishers should a technician know?
    3. When should each extinguisher be used?
    4. How is an extinguisher properly used?
Subject Content:
  A. Classification of Extinguishers (by materials for use with)
    1. Type A — common materials (wood, cloth, paper, rubber, some plastics)
    2. Type B — flammable liquids (gasoline, oil, grease, tar, lacquer, oil-based paints)
    3. Type C — functioning electrical equipment (wiring, fuse boxes, circuit breakers, machinery, appliances)
    4. Type D — Combustible metals (metal, alloy elements, metal dusts)
  B. Features to know
    1. Be familiar with location and type of extinguisher in workplace areas
    2. Higher the A&B rating number, more useful on larger fire
    3. See directions for use on label
  C. When to use a fire extinguisher
    1. After fire department has been called
    2. Extinguisher type is suitable for type of fire
    3. Fire is small and confined to area where it started
    4. Other people in area are evacuated
    5. Operator has safe evacuation route
  D. Operation of most extinguishers
    1. Pull pin
    2. Aim low
    3. Squeeze handle
    4. Sweep from side to side

As shown in the above example, questions for the topic direct the student to do more than memorize facts. The information learned must be used to make decisions and take actions to solve problems. **Always consider how to provide for the application of the information to be learned.**

Analyze a Performance Skill

When you prepare to teach **how to do** something, it is helpful to develop a step-by-step sequence like the following:

Subject area: WOOD TECHNOLOGY (Cabinetmaking)
Topic: Plastic Laminate on a Table Top

Procedure:
1. Cut laminate 1/4 inch larger than table top, on all sides
2. Sand table top surface smooth
3. Apply contact cement to back of laminate and table top
4. Allow cement to dry on both surfaces
5. Cover entire table top with wrapping paper
6. Align edge of laminate with one edge of the top; hold in place
7. Slide the paper out; press laminate down on top
8. Roll surface of laminate with wooden roller from center to edges in all directions
9. Remove excess laminate from edges
10. Clean excess adhesive from surface by scraping with piece of laminate

---

When analyzing a performance skill, consider these important facts:

- Often the skill is a complex task comprised of a number of **subtasks**. For example, to teach a person to swim the overhand crawl stroke, it is necessary to cover three subtasks: (1) arm movement, (2) leg kick, and (3) head movement while breathing. Then integrate the subtasks to perform the overall task.

- Analyze any skill to determine whether the sequence can be taught in step-by-step order, or whether it is necessary to consider one or more subtasks which themselves require a step-by-step sequence. Make certain the subtasks relate together, resulting in performance of the major skill. Also, as part of the procedure, decide whether use of special tools is needed.

- Learning a skill may also require learning and using information, like names and functions of parts, in addition to the physical movements.

The same procedure as described for selecting and organizing subject content can be used to specify a performance skill:

1. Write down **questions** about the information and procedure that students should answer or carry-out.
2. Arrange questions in logical, sequential order.
3. Outline the necessary information and details of the procedure in answer to each question. This may become a **checklist** as the student learns to perform the skill.

Here is an example of how a performance skill can be analyzed:

Topic: BENDING THERMOPLASTIC PIPE
Goal: To learn how to form thermoplastic piping into various radii bends with use of heat
Questions:
    1. What are advantages for using heat to bend thermoplastic pipe?
    2. How is length of pipe required for a bend determined?
    3. What techniques can be used to form a bend?
    4. What temperatures are necessary for heating PVC and CPVC piping?
    5. Why are pipe ends secured when heating piping?
    6. How can pipe be reinforced to maintain roundness when being heated?
Subject Content/Skill Details:
    A. Advantages of bending pipe with heat (**Content**)
        1. Eliminates use of fittings
        2. Reduces number of joints
        3. Eliminates sharp bends vulnerable to pressure surges
    B. Points to remember during bending (**Content**)
        1. Minimum radius of bend is 5-6 times pipe diameter
        2. Formula for minimum length pipe to cut for bend – $X = 0.0175 (A \times r)$
            X – mimimum bend portion of pipe length in inches
            A – angle subtending bent portion of pipe
            r – radius of bend in inches
        3. Jig is best means for accurately forming bend
        4. Target temperature — 270° F PVC; 300 F CPVC
        5. Use hand-held heater, not open flame for heat
        6. Secure pipe end to offset tendency of piping to creep out
    C. Reinforce inside of pipe to maintain roundness (**Content**)
        1. Fill pipe with fine sand, or
        2. Seal pipe ends with expandable plugs
    D. Bending procedure (**Skill**)
        1. Measure section to be bent for determining pipe length
        2. Reinforce pipe
        3. Apply heat to section for bending by moving heater evenly over pipe surface
        4. When softened, work at moderate speed to form radius or place in jig and bend
        5. Secure end of pipe until cooled
        6. Cool bend with water

Flowchart Outline

When teaching students to perform a skill, at certain points it may become necessary for them to make a decision, like a choice between two alternatives. Then, take appropriate action.

While decisions and branching steps can be shown in a list, as an alternate or to supplement, a **flowchart** outline can be helpful to the instructor during planning. This is a visual way to describe a task. For students, a flowchart can guide learning.

In a flowchart the following symbols are used:

 Beginning and end of the skill procedure

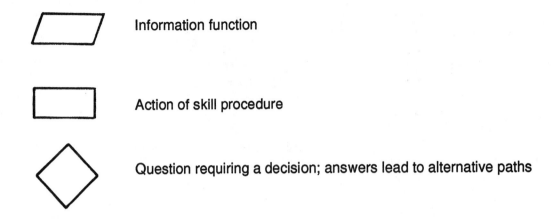

Information function

Action of skill procedure

Question requiring a decision; answers lead to alternative paths

Here is an example of a sequence list and related flowchart outline:

Project: TO JOIN METALS BY SOLDERING
Sequence List:
    A. Clean soldering iron
        1. File tip until bright copper
        2. Finish with steel wool
        3. Clean dirty tip with coarse steel wool
    B. Tin soldering iron
        1. Heat to maximum temperature (5 minutes)
        2. Apply flux-core solder over all sides
    C. Clean surface of pieces to be soldered with steel wool

Flowchart Diagram:

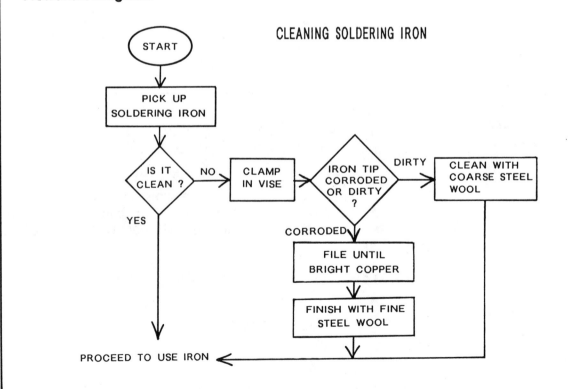

Although the flowchart may look complex, it represents how a person can think through the steps of a skill in a logical manner, decide where decision points are required, and set out alternative paths to consider. With this method, you focus on details that might be missed when just making a list of steps as a sequence to be followed. Then by giving students a copy of the procedural flowchart, they can quickly see the details of a sequence and the relationship among elements and alternatives.

Sources of Information

In order to outline content or describe a skill, you must have accurate and detailed information. While you may be knowledgeable and even an expert with the topic, it can be useful to check other sources to extend your knowledge and ensure accuracy and completeness. Sources for locating more information about a topic are:

- operating manuals, manufacturer's literature, texts, reports, and other printed materials
- video recordings, CD-ROM, and other resources used to present training on the topic
- observations and interviews with other persons who are known to have competence with the subject

Examine available sources. Take careful, detailed notes. Combine them with your own knowledge. Proceed to prepare the content outline and the skill sequence or flowchart.

Summary

1. A subject for training can be divided into one or more topics.

2. A task can be divided into a number of subtasks.

3. Based on topic and goal, a list of questions indicate what students should answer about the topic.

4. Content can be outlined and a skill sequenced as a list in response to questions.

5. A flowchart diagram can show the sequence of actions and decisions necessary for analyzing a skill.

6. Various sources, including publications, media resources, and content experts, can be used for gathering information about the topic.

Review Exercise

1. In what order would you apply the following initial steps for instructional planning on an assigned subject?
_____ a. Goal
_____ b. Sources of information
_____ c. Topics
_____ d. Content outline or skill details
_____ e. Subject
_____ f . Major questions

2. Classify each of the following according to these content levels:
    a). Facts, terms, definitions
    b). Descriptions, functions, processes
    c). Concepts, rules, principles, regulations, codes

_____ (1). An epoxy is a synthetic resin used in adhesive glues.
_____ (2). An antifreeze used in an automobile cooling system both lowers the freezing point and raises the boiling point of the coolant mixture.
_____ (3). Channel-type pliers can grasp larger objects than can slip-joint pliers.
_____ (4). In cutting the teeth of a worm wheel on a milling machine, two operations are required: gashing the teeth and hobbing the teeth to the correct size and shape.
_____ (5). A typical microprocessor can obey about 70 separate, simple instructions that can be combined to form powerful programs.

3. Below are initial planning items for a topic. Label each one according to the stages you answered for question 1 — goal, topic ...
(Note: Some items relate to planning **after** this chapter. Mark them with an X.)
    a. Hulls
       Decks
       Sails
       Propulsion systems
    b. Assign students to repair leaks in hulk-to-deck links
    c. To understand how a boat can be kept safe, good looking, and most useful
    d. Boat Maintenance and Repair
    e. Sails
       (1). Fibers
          (a). Dacron
          (b). Nylon
          (c). Mylar and Kevlar
       (2). Care
          (a). crease-free as possible
          (b). flake mains over boom, tie firmly
          (c). place each sail in a sail bag
          (d). clean with mild detergent at end of season
       (3). Repair
          (a). use round shaft needle for tears
          (b). use polyester thread
          (c). triple stitch all reinforcements
    f. Prepare diagrams to show --
       (1). stitching a seam with overhead stitch
       (2). securing patches with overhead stitch
       (3). closing tears with sailmaker's darn
    g. (1). What are the characteristics of four materials from which sails are made?
       (2). What care is necessary when handling a sail?
       (3). How are repairs made in a damaged sail?

4. Design a flowchart for the following:
    Task: Obtaining a cup of coffee from a vending machine
    Procedure:
       1. Read instructions on machine
       2. Put coins in slot (2 quarters)
       3. Decide — plain coffee, sugar, cream
       4. Push selection buttons

5. Take full cup from machine
6. If coffee doesn't pour, press coin return and try again
7. If machine is not working properly push coin return button, take coins and leave

5. What are two supplementary sources for information you might use to obtain or check the content for a training topic?

Answers: 1. a – 2; b – 5; c – 3; d – 6; e – 1 ; f – 4.
2. a – 1; b – 4,5; c – 2,3.
3. a – topics; b – X (instruction); c – goal; d – subject; e – content outline;
   f – X (resources); g – questions.
4. (See below)
5. Printed materials: manuals, texts, reports, manufacturer's publications.
   Media materials: films, video recordings.
   Observing or interviewing other experts.

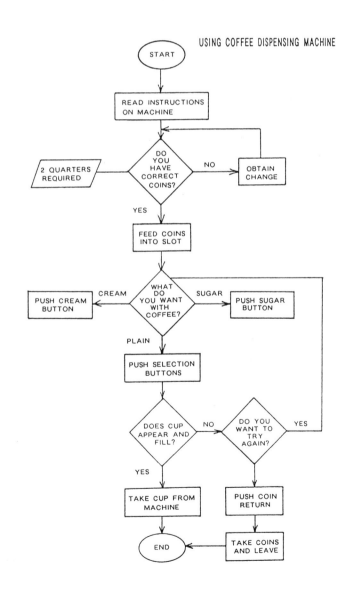

USING COFFEE DISPENSING MACHINE

References

Analyzing Instructional Content: A Guide to Instruction and Evaluation. P. Tiemann and S. Markle. Champaign, IL: Stipes Publishing, 1985.

Analyzing Jobs and Tasks. K. E. Carlisle. Englewood Cliffs, NJ: Educational Technology Publications, 1986.

Designing Effective Instruction and Learning. J. E. Kemp and others. Columbus, OH: Macmillan, 1993.

Developing Vocational Instruction. R. F. Mager and K. M. Beach. Belmont, CA: Lake Publisher, 1984.

Essentials of Learning for Instruction. R. M. Gagne and M. P. Driscoll. Englewood Cliffs, NJ: Prentice-Hall, 1988.

Everything You Always Wanted to Know About Job Analysis. E. Levine. Tampa, FL: Mariner Publishing, 1983.

"Flowchart Primer." D. Cram. *Training and Development Journal*, 1980, *34* (7), 64-68.

Goal Analysis. R. F. Mager. Belmont, CA: Fearon/Pitman, 1984.

"A Review of Strategies for Sequencing and Synthesizing Instruction." L. Van Patten, C. Chao, and C. Reigeluth. *Review of Educational Research,* 1986, *56*, 437-471.

"Task Analysis." S. Jackson in *Introduction to Performance Technology.* M. Smith, ed. Washington, DC: National Society for Performance and Instruction, 1986.

"What Is a Task?" D. Reddout. *Performance and Instruction,* 1987, *26* (1), 5-6.

Chapter 3

HOW DO I WRITE OBJECTIVES?

In this chapter you will learn to:

- **Recognize the importance of learning object- ives in training.**
- **Relate learning objectives to subject content.**
- **Identify the three domains of learning object- ives.**
- **Write learning objectives consisting of up to four parts.**
- **Prepare to inform students of objectives for which they will be responsible.**

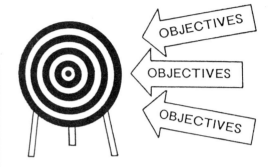

Many instructors are familiar with the subject of objectives. In your profession, you have had many specific assignments or tasks to perform. In each instance, you were most likely told what the objective to be accomplished would be. You went ahead with your plans, or the operation accordingly.

Importance of Learning Objectives

The purpose of training is to provide for satisfactory learning by the student. Therefore, we use the expression **learning objectives** for this element of planning. Other terms often used are **instructional objectives**, **behavioral objectives**, or **performance objectives**. They all have the same meaning.

Objectives are necessary for these reasons:

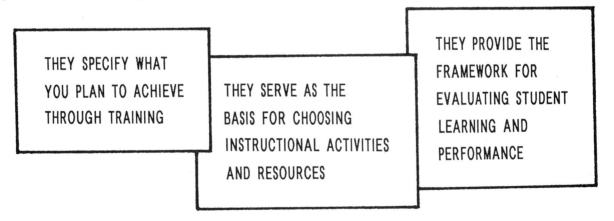

Not only are objectives important to the instructor, but they also inform students precisely what is required of them. Thus, they help the student know what to study and how to prepare for tests. There is positive evidence that students who are informed of the learning objectives they are to satisfy do have greater success in learning than do those not so informed.

Learning Objectives and Subject Content

The questions, along with the subject content or skill details for a topic, provide information from which learning objectives can be derived. For example:

Subject: ELECTRONIC DIGITAL TECHNIQUES
Goal: To become familiar with features of digital signals in electronics

Questions:
  1. What is the difference between analog and digital signals?
  2. What devices operate with either analog or digital signals?
  3. In what electronics areas are digital techniques applied?
  4. What are advantages of using digital techniques?

Subject Content:
  A. Difference between analog and digital signals
       1. Analog signals move smoothly or continuously
       2. Digital signals pulse between two fixed levels
  B. Difference between analog and digital devices
       1. Analog devices
            a. automobile speedometer
            b. TV volume control
            c. conventional clock
            d. standard multimeter
       2. Digital devices
            a. automobile multimeter
            b. TV VHF channel selector
            c. clock with decimal number display
       3. Uses for digital techniques
            ....
       4. Advantages of digital techniques
            ....
Objectives: The student will be able to:
  1. describe the difference between analog and digital signals
  2. classify devices as either of analog or digital type
  3. select areas of electronics that use digital techniques
  4. list five advantages of digital techniques

When an instructor is very familiar with the subject content and skill procedure for a topic, objectives may be prepared **before** listing the content or skill details. In such an instance, it is recommended that following the objectives, the content/skill items be written out to verify that:

  • all content and skill items for the topic are included;
  • the content and procedures are organized and logically sequenced;
  • there is a close relationship between content/procedure and objectives.

Writing Learning Objectives

A learning objective is a precise statement that indicates a competency students should acquire in order to perform satisfactorily on the job.

An objective answers the question — **"What should the student know, or be able to do, or what new behavior should be evident as the result of training in this topic?"** Examine the content and ask yourself this question each time you start to formulate an objective. The answer will guide you in writing your learning objectives.

A learning objective may consist of up to four parts:

> An **action verb** that describes the learning required:
> **recognize, describe, apply, practice, collect**

> The **content** or **skill** component of the topic:
> **single-pass heat exchanger, hydraulic system, basic ECL circuit, band saw**

> The required **performance level** of learning:
> **at least 4 out of 5, 90% accuracy, meeting criteria, within 3 minutes, in proper order**

> Any **conditions** under which learning is to take place:
> **with special equipment, simulated or realistic conditions, along with a partner, using the manual, something denied when performing the task**

The first two parts — **action verb** and **content or skill** component — are **essential** in each statement of an objective, while the other two parts — **performance level** and **conditions** — may be desirable but may be considered as **optional** for inclusion as appropriate.

By referring to these four parts, objectives can be accurately stated to represent the learning needed. Also, they clearly inform students of what will be required of them. Here is an example:

> Given a two-stroke motorcycle engine, be able to measure excessive crankshaft wear with 90% accuracy

Special Awareness When Writing Objectives

You should keep two thoughts in mind as you write your learning objectives. First, instructors and even students may confuse objectives and goals. As explained near the beginning of Chapter 2, a goal is a general statement that indicates what will be accomplished for the topic.

Example:

> **Topic:** INDUSTRIAL ROBOTS
> **Goal:** To know how robots function in production automation
> **Objective:** When supplied with Milacron equipment, to install robots for assembly operation that fully meet procedural criteria

As you now see, **learning objectives are specific and detailed.** They clearly describe the expected learning outcomes by students.

The second important thing to keep in mind as you prepare to write objectives is that, in some topics there is such a natural, close relationship between elements of knowledge or skill components. The instructor might like to use **two** action verbs in a single objective (example: to

select a drill bit and **drill** a hole). This should be avoided. Each activity should be considered separately and sequentially learned. Therefore, limit each objective to one verb, signifying a single learning requirement.

For the above example:

> To select a drill bit for required hole size
> To drill a hole with the ABC drill press

Categories of Objectives

All objectives for learning can be grouped into three major categories often called **domains —
cognitive, psychomotor,** and **affective.** They indicate the form of learning as indicated below:

- The **cognitive** domain includes objectives for learning information (example: **classification of logic circuits**) and carrying out thought processes (example: **deciding on need to replace a noisy motor**).

- The **psychomotor** domain treats physical skills requiring the use of muscles to do something (examples: **use a reciprocating saw, solder copper fittings**).

- The **affective** domain involves attitudes, personal feelings, and interpersonal relations that are often called the "soft skills" (examples: **maintain clean work area, persist at solving technical problems**).

Although we consider each of the three domains separately, they are closely related. When you examine a topic, often more than a single domain requires attention (like cognitive/ psychomotor for the plastic pipe example on page 15). In preparation for writing learning objectives, you need to identify the types of learning you will require within each domain.

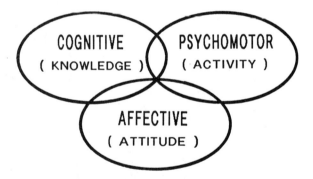

Cognitive Domain Objectives that treat informational topics (cognitive domain) may start with verbs like: to **recognize**, to **assess**, to **classify**, and to **arrange.** To the verb is added the necessary content component.

Here are examples of cognitive domain objectives:

> To recognize the three parts of a basic pneumatic system
> To assess the potential health hazards in an electrochemical plant
> To classify the types of corrosion found in boiler equipment
> To arrange the dismantling steps of a motorcycle engine

Careful selection of the proper verb to indicate the required learning is the most important part of objective writing. You will find a helpful list of verbs below. Note the first column of words — **define, label, list, name,** and so on. They indicate the **recall** or **memorization** of information. Words in the other columns — **analyze, describe, plan,** and so forth, require **understanding, using the information, solving problems,** and **making decisions.** A successful training program should include many objectives with higher level verbs like those in the three right-side columns.

Verbs Useful in Writing Cognitive Learning Objectives

define	analyze	describe	plan
label	apply	evaluate	predict
list	arrange	explain	relate
name	assess	interpret	report
order	calculate	judge	review
recognize	categorize	locate	select
repeat	choose	manage	solve
reproduce	compare	organize	use

Now as necessary, add either or both of the other two parts to complete each learning objective the required **performance level** of learning, and any **conditions.**

Here are examples: (For illustrative purposes, a single underline indicates the required performance level; a dashed underline marks the condition under which the objective is to be accomplished.)

- To recognize the three parts of a basic pneumatic system with 100% accuracy

- Using the IHF manual, to assess potential health hazards in an electrochemical plant according to listed criteria

- To classify, according to company procedure, the types of corrosion found in boiler equipment with no errors

- Given a British two-stroke motorcycle engine, to arrange the dismantling steps in proper order

---

Psychomotor Domain

Much of the procedure explained for writing cognitive domain objectives also applies to preparing psychomotor objectives. Verbs that indicate physical actions — **load, operate, perform,** and **direct** — are descriptive of required learning (called "hard skills"). To the verb add a procedural phrase for the skill.

Here are examples of psychomotor domain objectives:

To repair a plastic pipe system
To use a dado blade to make lap joints
To adjust timing in a marine diesel engine
To test a water pump for correct operating pressure

Each craft has its own particular skill requirements. Sample verbs are listed below.

Verbs Useful in Writing Psychomotor Learning Objectives

adjust	identify	operate
bend	(an odor)	perform
differentiate	handle	repair
(by touch)	measure	taste
grasp	move	use

As explained, the choice of the verb should clearly describe the action to be performed. Add the required performance standard for successful accomplishment, and any conditions important when the performance takes place.

Here are examples: (Single underline: performance standard; dashed underline: condition)

- To repair a plastic pipe system according to company procedure and fully meeting state requirements

- To use a dado blade to make a lap joint as specified by five safety actions

- With reference to Table 5-2, to adjust valve timing in a marine diesel engine with 100% accuracy

- To test a Cooper water pump for correct operating pressure within a 10 minute period

---

Affective Domain

This category of learning objectives is important in technical training for the formation and development of attitudes and values (also called **soft skills**) by an individual, either as a student, or employee. It also refers to how a person relates to other individuals in various interpersonal situations. Verbs like **respect, obey, support,** and **cooperate** can be used.

Verbs Useful in Writing Affective Domain Objectives

agree	engage in	participate in
assist	help	praise
assume responsibility	is attentive to	respect
avoid	join	share
cooperate	offer	support

Although individual behavior is the best way that an attitude may be shown, the accomplishment of affective domain objectives cannot always be easily observed. Attitude formation is an internal and private matter for an individual. Thus, it may be difficult to know when an attitude is acquired and becomes overtly evident to other persons as the result of training.

Successful development of an attitude needs to be recognized from behavior changes. For example, how do you determine successful accomplishment in training for this objective?

> To cooperate as a team member in carrying out assigned tasks

Satisfactory accomplishment can be recognized from clues like these:

- Reports to work promptly at starting time
- Assists others with their work when requested
- Volunteers to help others
- Avoids sexual harassment implications
- Offers suggestions when confronting a problem situation
- Commends others on quality of their work

When developing affective domain objectives, always consider the types of behaviors, like those above, that would have to be exhibited as proof of their accomplishment. You might treat this list of clues as a "subject content" outline for an affective learning objective.

Inform Students of Required Objectives

At the beginning of this chapter it was indicated that learning objectives also are important to students. Therefore at the start of training, or when beginning a new topic, give students a list of required learning objectives. They will know what is specifically required of them and by what standards their learning will be evaluated.

Summary

1. Learning objectives direct the selection of instructional activities and resources, and specify the way to test student learning.

2. Learning objectives most often are derived from subject content.

3. Learning objectives consist of up to four parts — verb, content component, performance standard, and condition. The first two are essential, and the others are optional.

4. While a goal is a general statement for a topic, learning objectives are specific outcomes for learning.

5. Learning objectives are grouped into three domains: cognitive (information), psychomotor (skill), and affective (attitudes and interpersonal relations).

6. The accomplishment of affective domain objectives can be evident from identified behavior clues.

7. A topic may include learning objectives in more than one domain.

8. Students should be informed of the objectives they will be expected to accomplish.

Review Exercise

1. Which of the following statements are NOT true with respect to learning objectives?
___ a. They help you decide how to teach the content for a topic.
___ b. They indicate the broad goal of a training program.
___ c. They indicate how to test learning.
___ d. They direct students in their study.
___ e. They state what the trainer's responsibilities are.

2. Which of the following words would you choose for use when writing a learning objective.
___ a. to know   ___ d. to summarize   ___ g. to list
___ b. to relate   ___ e. to learn   ___ h. to become aware of
___ c. to calculate   ___ f . to understand   ___ i . to apply

3. Name each of the parts of the following learning objective:

With reference to a Cytex controller, program a robotic seam welding system having a maximum output error of 1.5mm.

4. Examine the list of objectives below; then answer the questions that follow.

a. To describe all grounding requirements for residential electrical wiring as specified in the National Electrical Code.

b. Having available a spur gear index chart, machine a pair of matching spur gears according to assigned ratios.

c. To identify five abrasive grits used in sanding procedures.

d. To solder connections.

e. To calculate the cost for materials and labor to repair a two-stroke small engine.

f. To maintain a clean and neat assigned working area.

(1). Into which category of learning objectives (cognitive, psychomotor, affective) would you classify each one?

(2). Which one(s) in the cognitive domain require high level comprehension rather than simple recall of information?

(3). Which <u>one</u> objective is not completely worded?

Answers: 1. b.   2. b,c,d,g,i.
         3. **verb**: program, **subject**: robotic seam welding system, **performance standard:** maximum output error of 1.5mm, **condition**: with reference to a Cytex controller.
         4. (1)cognitive: a,c,e; psychomotor: b,d; affective: f.
             (2) a,e. (3) d.

References

The Affective and Cognitive Domains: Integration for Instruction and Research. B. L. Martin and L.J. Briggs. Englewood Cliffs, NJ: Educational Technology Publications, 1986.

How to Write Instructional Objectives. N. Gronlund. New York: Macmillan, 1990.

Preparing Instructional Objectives. R. F. Mager. Belmont, CA: David Lake, Publisher, 1984.

"Setting Objectives." In *Instructing and Evaluating in Higher Education*. R. J. McBeath, ed. Englewood Cliffs, NJ: Educational Technology Publications, 1992.

Taxonomy of Educational Objectives: Cognitive Domain. B. S. Bloom and others. New York: Longman, 1956.

Taxonomy of Educational Objectives: Affective Domain. D. R. Krathwohl and others. New York: Longman, 1964.

Taxonomy of the Psychomotor Domain. A. J. Harrow. New York: Longman, 1979.

Chapter 4

WHO ARE MY STUDENTS?

In this chapter you will learn to:

- Recognize the importance of determining student preparation for training.
- Identify the basic strengths of each class member.
- Recognize that student learning styles do vary.
- Gather information as to students' readiness for training in the subject.
- Determine prerequisites that each student should have in preparation for studying the subject.
- Find out what students already know about the subject.
- Assess unique features of adults as students.

INSTRUCTOR   INSTRUCTOR

Have you ever been a student in a training situation in which you felt frustrated because you did not have the necessary background to understand the material being presented? Or, as an instructor, have you discovered that a number of the students come with limited useful knowledge appropriate to the subject.

Are these concerns important ... both to the instructor and to students? Most certainly they are! With the variety of individuals in technical vocations, it cannot be assured that each person has the knowledge and skills to successfully start studying a topic.

Therefore, there are benefits to finding out as much as you can about the students in your class. You should:

- Adjust your training to take into account the variations you find in student preparation.
- Assist students better to prepare themselves for the training.

Background Experience

KNOW YOUR LEARNERS

Learn as much as you can about each student who will be in your class. If yours is a college course, academic records should be available. This can reveal educational level and other information about each individual's background.

If such information may be important and cannot be obtained from records, then you may want to prepare a brief questionnaire that includes the following:

1. What is your present job or anticipated position?
2. What is the highest education level you have successfully attained?
3. In what subject or subjects have you been the strongest?
4. What experiences have you had that prepare you for this course?

Distribute the questionnaire prior to the start of training, or have it completed during the first class meeting. The results can provide useful data that may affect your lesson plans and what assistance you may want to give individuals for their better preparation.

Be alert to any student for whom English is a second language. The use of illustrations or other media during instruction can provide understanding when English is limited. See Section B.

Also, recognize that some students may have disabilities that require special consideration during training. This may be a physical handicap, a degree of blindness, or hearing difficulties. Check with a personnel counselor or human resources development (HRD) staff for suggestions on how to work with such persons.

Learning Styles

People differ in how they engage in thinking, learning, and problem solving. Each student probably finds certain methods of study and learning more appealing and effective for them than other ways. This is referred to as a person's **learning style**. For a long time it has been known that, in preference to verbal lectures or reading material, some individuals learn better from visual materials, and others from physical activities or the manipulation of objects.

Another aspect of learning styles has to do with how people prefer to study and learn. There are those who would rather learn by themselves, while other persons prefer to learn through group activities, or in a lecture situation.

A CLASS WILL CONTAIN PEOPLE WHO LEARN BEST FROM DIFFERENT KINDS OF EXPERIENCES

Determining learning style preferences is not a definite science. But try to recognize that this important factor of difference among your students does exist. Do this by planning to provide for more than a single instructional activity as alternative ways to treat a topic. For example, you may decide to show the class a video recording to accompany a lecture. Some students may acquire a better understanding of the subject from the video than from the verbal presentation. As you will see in Chapter 5, there are alternatives to conventional classroom instruction that also can serve different learning styles.

Attitude Toward Subject

Students may come to a class with a well-defined attitude about the subject. They may even have a strong belief concerning the need or value for the training itself! Thus, it may become necessary to emphasize the importance of the topics, or otherwise motivate an interest in studying the subject.

While you may be able to get a "feeling" for individuals' beliefs with a brief open discussion, a preferable method is to develop another short questionnaire and obtain student responses (unsigned). Tabulations of the replies will reveal how you might approach the subject.

Here are types of questions that can be used to gather data about attitudes and beliefs:

---

1. Which statement do you select?
___ a. I am looking forward to this class.
___ b. I was assigned to take this course, but do not know
     if it is necessary.
___ c. The subject of this class may be a waste of time.
___ d. I have no opinion at this time.

2. This subject is important to my job. (Mark along the line.)

Strongly agree	Agree	Neutral	Disagree	Strongly disagree

3. Which words describe your attitude and expectations for this class:

___enthusiastic	___unhappy	___interested
___bored	___excited	___doubtful
___uncertain	___pleased	___disinterested

4. I would like to see the following happen in this course:

Competencies Relating to Subject

In addition to basic abilities and attitudes about the subject, it is important to find out what knowledge and skills students already possess as related to the subject. There are two parts to this:

- Background or preparation and motivation that a student has for studying the subject or topic (called **prerequisite** knowledge, skills, or attitudes).
- Knowledge and skill the student may already have **with the objectives** for the subject.

It is useful to determine the level of each student's background for, and competence with, the subject. You can do this by having students complete a **pretest**. This would include both prerequisite and topic-to-be-studied questions.

For example, on the topic of **Diesel Electrical Power Plant**, a **prerequisite** question might be:

> Describe, in one or more drawings, how a 4-cycle gasoline engine operates.

For the same topic, treating the objective: **To differentiate between a diesel and a gasoline engine**, in order to determine competency a student might already have, a **pretest** question might be:

> State the basic difference between a diesel engine and a gasoline engine.

The pretest usually is developed after the posttest (final exam) for the subject has been prepared. At that time, questions can be selected or adapted from the final exam. Look over the learning objectives for the topic. Decide about prerequisite requirements and what should be tested.

Inform students as to the purpose of the pretest — **to assist both instructor and student in better preparing for learning.** Tell students the test will not be graded. They should attempt their best, but not to guess just to try for correct answers.

Finally, the results of a pretest can help the instructor to add or modify some objectives or activities to take into account student preparation level for learning. It may be necessary to provide some assistance or assign special self-study activity when important deficiencies are found.

Special Features of Adult Learners

The students in technical training generally are adults. They are mature, and should be treated accordingly. Here are some unique characteristics of adults that are important considerations in training:

- Adults enter a training program with a high level of motivation to learn. They appreciate a program that is structured systematically, with requirements (objectives) clearly specified.
- Adults want to know how the class will benefit them. They expect the material to be relevant, and they quickly grasp the practical use of the content.
- To adults, time is an important consideration. They expect the class to start and finish on schedule. They do not like to waste time.
- Adults respect an instructor who is fully knowledgeable about the subject and presents it effectively. Students quickly detect an unprepared instructor.
- Adults bring to a class extensive experience from their personal and working lives. These experiences should be used as major resources by helping students relate to the subject being studied.
- Most mature adults are self-directed and independent. While some adults lack

confidence and need reassurance, they would prefer that the instructor serve as facilitator to guide and assist, rather than one who acts as an authoritarian leader.

- Adults want to participate in decision-making. They want to cooperate with the instructor in mutual assessment of needs and goals, in the choice of activities, and in deciding on evidence for evaluating learning.
- Adults may be less flexible than are younger students. Their habits and methods of operation have been developed into a routine. They do not like to be placed in embarrassing situations. Before they accept a new or changed way for doing something, they would want to know an advantage for doing so.
- Adults also like to cooperate in groups and socialize together. Provide for small group activities and an atmosphere for interaction during break are important. Also, be available to students during work sessions and outside of class yourself.

These characteristics of adults, along with variations in learning styles, and recognizing principles from learning psychology (page 135), make it apparent that individuals should be helped to become self-directed learners. This means that the instructor should not make all decisions about how and when to learn. In comparison to conventional teaching, a flexible, more open mode of instruction needs to be considered. With newer technologies, or by adapting regular media forms for self-paced learning (see Chapter 14), students can be guided to become individualized learners.

Summary

1. Determining basic competencies of students can indicate the level at which instruction should begin.

2. Determining student learning styles can help an instructor make learning effective for each person.

3. Determining student attitudes toward the subject can help an instructor introduce the subject so as to motivate an interest in it.

4. Determining student knowledge of prerequisites for studying a subject, and competencies with knowledge and skills relating to the subject, can be done with pretest questions.

5. Pretest results can help students ready themselves for training, and can help the instructor adjust procedures for more successful results.

6. Recognizing special features of adults can help an instructor to be better prepared for working successfully with students.

Review Exercise

1. You are designing a training program on the topic of: **Benchtop Metalworking.** Classify the following items according to the various categories presented in this chapter.

_____ a. What kind of metal is used in each sample on display?

_____ b. How important do you think this subject is in machine shop practice?

_____ c. For the topic of **How to Use a Tap** (tool for cutting a thread inside a hole), have available: descriptive reading material, set of photographs showing steps in procedure, and video recording of procedure.

____ d. Describe three ways that two pieces of metal can be attached together.

2. How can you take into account different learning styles of students?

3. Which statements are TRUE relative to adult students.

___ a. End a class session at scheduled time.

___ b. Do not talk down to students.

___ c. Students can figure out for themselves the relevance of content being presented.

___ d. Provide students with the learning objectives for the topic.

___ e. Adults prefer being in regular size classes for most instruction.

___ f . Most trainers can cover themselves when unprepared for a class so students cannot detect this deficiency.

Answers: 1. a – prerequisite (background information), b – attitude, c – recognizing different learning styles, d – pretest (knowledge of topic).
2. Provide more than one way to learn about a topic (talk, visuals, physical activity).
3. a,b,d.

References

The Adult Learner: A Neglected Species. M. Knowles. Houston, TX: Gulf Publishing, 1984.

"Assessing Your Learning Style." L. Stephen. In *The Trainer's Professional Development Handbook.* R. Bard, ed. San Francisco: Jossey-Bass, 1987.

Developing Attitude Toward Learning. R. F. Mager. Belmont, CA: David Lake, Publisher, 1984.

"Developing Opinion, Interest, and Attitude Questionnaires." In *Instructing and Evaluating in Higher Education.* R. J. McBeath, ed. Englewood Cliffs, NJ: Educational Technology Publications, 1992.

"Diagnosing Learning Styles." G. Price. In *Helping Adults Learn How to Learn.* R. M. Smith, ed. San Francisco: Jossey-Bass, 1983.

Enhancing Adult Motivation to Learn. R. J. Wlodkowski. San Francisco: Jossey-Bass, 1985.

Learning How to Learn: Applied Learning Theory for Adults. R. Smith. New York: Cambridge Books, 1982.

"Learning to Learn." D. Maxfield and R.M. Smith. In *Materials and Methods in Adult and Continuing Education.* C. Klevins, ed. Los Angeles: Klevins, 1987.

Learning Style Inventory: A Self Description of Preferred Learning Modes. D. A. Kolb. Boston: McBer, 1978.

The Modern Practice of Adult Education. M. S. Knowles. Englewood Cliffs, NJ: Cambridge Press, 1988.

"Multicultural Training: Designing for Affective Results." H. D. Stolovitch and M. Lane. *Performance and Instruction,* 1989, *28*(6), 10-15.

People Types and Tiger Stripes: A Practical Guide to Learning Styles. Gainesville, FL: Center for Applications of Psychological Types, 1982.

"30 Things We Know for Sure About Adult Learning." R. Zemke and S. Zemke. **Training,** 1988, *25*(7), 57-61.

Chapter 5

HOW CAN I DO THE TRAINING?

In this chapter you will learn to:

> • Recognize that all methods of training can be grouped into three broad categories.
> • Identify the features, advantages, and limitations of activities in each category.
> • Relate examples for training in each category.
> • Identify the features, advantages, and disadvantages of on-the job training.

Often an instructor believes that unless he or she is in front of the class talking, demonstrating, showing, or otherwise presenting information, no learning can take place. This is not correct. While many instructors are most comfortable with lecturing, there is a number of alternative training methods you might consider using. Once you become familiar with them, you may find some more effective in accomplishing certain learning objectives.

As indicated in Chapter 4, students differ in their learning styles. Therefore, by varying the instructional methods you use, you can better provide for these differences in approaches to learning by individuals.

Two other important concerns relate closely to the successful application of the training methods we examine in this chapter. First is recognition that technical training can take place on four levels of learning:

1. **Memorizing facts** that need to be recalled on the job.
2. **Understanding generalizations** like concepts, rules, processes, and procedures that

are used in fulfilling job responsibilities.
3. **Developing physical skills** required in job performance.
4. **Using** and **applying** the above **learning** to job functions including solving practical problems and making decisions.

Second, in order to accomplish these four levels of learning, there are important principles and practices derived from learning theory that should be applied. They are treated near the beginning of Chapter 15 when instructional planning is summarized and lesson plans are being prepared. Give those elements careful attention as you select instructional methods and specify learning activities.

Categories of Teaching and Learning Methods

There are three broad ways in which instruction can take place:

- **Presentation** to a class
- **Self-paced learning** for individual students
- **Small group** activities

Each category has certain features and can be advantageous for accomplishing specific goals. Both the requirements of a topic's learning objectives and an instructor's teaching preference will determine which methods might be used at various times, either separately or in combination.

For technical training, a common procedure is to present information in the classroom and then send students to a laboratory, shop, or production area to apply and practice what was learned. In other situations, a classroom session may be followed by one-to-one on-the-job training. In either case, the training consists of a combination of teaching and learning activities selected from the above three broad groups. While we now consider each category separately, they are frequently integrated in actual use.

Presentation to a Class

In the presentation category, the instructor communicates information to students, usually by lecturing and showing audiovisual materials. This is frequently called the **platform technique.** Listening to a speaker, viewing slides or overhead transparencies shown by the instructor, or watching a video recording are all presentation methods. When such activities are used, they illustrate the transmission of information from **instructor to students**.

Advantages   The benefits of a presentation method include the following:

- Because lecturing is so widely used, it is easy to continue the habit and students are accustomed to it.
- In relation to other instructional methods, less effort may be required to plan a lecture or a media presentation.
- Instructional time may be saved because more information can be presented in a given time period than by other methods.
- Large numbers of students can be served at one time; the group limited

only by the size of the room, or the reach of a television broadcasting facility (called *distance learning*).

- It is a flexible method when information requires changes, updating, or adapting for a specific group.

Limitations
- Students are confined to passive learning by listening and watching; only taking notes. Unless questions and comments by students are encouraged, there would be limited overt participation for learning. Thus, this method could violate many learning principles presented in Chapter 15.
- Not all instructors can be good lecturers ... always interesting, enthusiastic, and challenging in order to maintain student attention during the presentation.
- When an instructor presents subject content, the assumption is made that all students acquire the same level of understanding, at the same time. They are forced to learn at the pace set by the instructor. We know this is not the way learning actually takes place.
- Each person learns according to his or her own learning style and preparation for the topic. (Recall pretesting, as described in Chapter 4, as a way to determine preparation and experience levels of students.)
- It is sometimes difficult for the instructor to obtain feedback from students as to misunderstandings encountered during the presentation. Therefore, some students may leave class with incorrect learning.
- There is evidence that the content of a purely verbal presentation, with no planned student participation, is remembered for only a short time.

Applications
Of the four learning levels listed on page 39, only memorizing and understanding are appropriate for the presentation method. Here are situations and times for which a presentation to a class can be of most value:

- To introduce a new topic, or provide an overview or orientation for a topic.
- To serve as motivation for creating interest in a new subject.
- To present basic or essential information as background or necessary preparation before other individual or group activity.
- To introduce new content when instructor preparation time is limited.
- To provide such resources as a guest speaker, a video recording, or other visual presentation that can most conveniently or efficiently be shown to all members of the class at one time.
- To provide opportunities for students to make reports of their own to the class.
- As a review or summary when study of a topic is concluded.

Carefully weigh the advantages and limitations of the presentation method of training in terms of learning objectives to be accomplished. Then, if a presentation is feasible, decide on the form it should take — verbal lecture, lecture with supporting media, or media alone.

Plan for Participation
Keep in mind that learning takes place best when students are actively involved, not just sitting passively receiving the information. Therefore, it is important to plan for participation activities during a presentation, like the following:

- Prepare questions to be used at various points during the presentation. Invite or direct selected students to answer and to engage in discussion.
- Encourage note-taking by students so they write down the key points being presented; or provide handouts for reference and immediate use. These may be worksheets with questions or problems, an outline to be completed, or a diagram to be constructed.
- Urge students to think along with you by helping them to mentally answer rhetorical questions you periodically ask. These are questions you ask but do not expect anyone to answer out loud — "Do you see how Part A relates to Part B?"
- For further suggestions on formulating questions see page 45.

Self-Paced Learning

Learning is a process that must be accomplished by the individual. There can be advantages for having students work individually, each at his or her own pace, actively involved in completing specific assignments. This can be reading, viewing media, completing worksheets, solving problems, practicing a skill, or carrying out other self-paced activities.

Features   Self-paced learning often includes the following:

- Content to be learned is organized into logical sequences, each one treating a section of the topic.
- Individual activities and resources are selected to match the required learning objectives.
- Accomplishment of objectives by the student is tested before proceeding to the next sequence.
- Immediate confirmation (feedback) of test results is provided to the student. With success, the student proceeds to the next section. Without acceptable success, the student may restudy and/or receive help, then be tested again.
- Each of the four learning levels beginning on page 39 can be served by the self-paced learning pattern.

Advantages   There is evidence that students participating in self-paced learning activities work harder, may learn more, and are apt to retain what has been learned better than do students in conventional classes. Also, self-paced learning experiences can prepare an individual to become more self-directed and a more responsible person in further training and work experiences.

Limitations   Note these important limitations to self-paced learning:

- Requires careful planning for the development of self-study materials.
- Requires variety in activities and resources so the same routine is not repeatedly followed in a lengthy training program that could become monotonous.
- Requires extra equipment, multiple copies of materials, and suitable facilities.
- May require new habits for study to be formed by some students to overcome lack of self-discipline or procrastination.
- May require qualified personnel available to assist students while studying.

Applications Here are some commonly used formats for self-paced learning. (See Chapter 15 for further explanations):

• **Textbook/Manual with Visuals and Worksheets**
Students can be directed to read a section or chapter of a reference; study illustrations on paper, view slides or a video recording. Then they answer questions to check and apply their understanding of the content. After completion, the students should be better prepared to use the knowledge learned for other activities.

Example –

> **Student Group:** Entry level semi-skilled employees in electronic company
> **Topic**: Microprocessor Fundamentals

• **Job Aid**
When details of a task may be complex or difficult to re-member, a job aid can be used for reference. The job aid can be directions to operate equipment, to carry-out a procedure, or to troubleshoot a problem. Information and instructions could be on paper, as a diagram, a card, a set of photographs or slides with an audiotaped narr-ation, a video recording, even as a computer software program, or any combination of these resources.

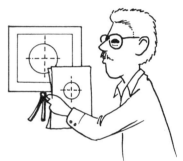

The detailed instructions can replace repetitive explanations or demonstrations that an instructor may have to give frequently. After introductory instruction, a job aid can be referred to by a worker thereafter, whenever necessary.

Example –

> **Student Group:** Air Conditioning Technicians
> **Job Aid**: Sequence list to review of maintenance procedures
>   for five heat pump models

• **Computer-Based Training (CBT)**
A computer program can be a dynamic way to guide a student in learning about a topic. The student may select the point at which to start the program or, by being pretested, the program could direct the student where to start. Progress through the program can be in a linear order (studying content in 1,2,3... sequence). Or, the student may be branched to review, repeat, or skip ahead.

Frequently the student responds to questions or problems that test understanding. Knowledge of results is provided immediately.

Example –

> **Student Group**: Electronics company operating technicians
> **Example**: CBT to teach window-based computer applications

In addition to the computer program, with proper equipment and software, still pictures and video material can be integrated and presented. See Chapter 14 for further information about computer and multimedia uses in training.

Example –

> **Student Group**: Field Technicians
> **Subject**:   New procedures (computer-controlled videodisc
>   program) for servicing and repairing robots in small
>   manufacturing facilities

Self-paced learning can provide the flexibility to serve specific training needs of individuals. In small-size organizations, or in situations when employees are widely dispersed, it may not be logistically possible (or desirable) to conduct formal lecture classes for staff. In such situations, self-paced learning activities, with necessary resources, may be very appropriate.

Conventional and new-type resources can allow for flexible learning at many off-worksite locations. Resources may include the telephone, electronic mail, the fax machine, the computer with its modem for external communication, two-way video, and so on. Careful detail should be given to preparing or gathering self-instructional materials, as well as in providing supervision for training, and evaluating the resulting student competency.

As with other forms of instruction, it is important to document student learning as the result of self-paced learning activities. Careful records should be kept of the accomplishments by each student.

Small Group Activities

In this third teaching/learning category, the instructor and students, or students themselves, discuss, question, practice, apply, and otherwise pursue learning cooperatively. Students working in groups can be most effective when scheduled to follow an instructor-led presentation to a class or self-paced learning activities.

With reference to the four levels of learning listed on pages 39-40 knowledge and skills that have already been learned can be reviewed, clarified, reinforced, and applied through group activities. Students would be able to learn from each other as well as from the instructor.

Advantages   In comparison with the presentation and self-paced learning categories, there are unique features:

- They can better achieve objectives in the affective domain than can procedures in other teaching/learning categories.

- Higher-level intellectual skills, like applications, problem-solving, and decision-making, can receive special emphasis.
- Experiences in listening and speaking enable students to strengthen their own learning as they offer explanations and reactions to the positions taken by others.
- Experiences in cooperation and mutual support among students prepare them for similar behavior on the job.
- Students who need encouragement can be recognized and those who are making poor progress can be identified.

Special Matters

In order to make group activities successful, the instructor should make an effort to ensure that:

- all students come prepared;
- all students are encouraged to participate;
- no one should be permitted to monopolize a discussion or control an activity ... including the instructor!

Applications

Various techniques may be used to encourage and provide for activities within groups of students:

- **Instructor/Student Discussion**

This is the most common form of face-to-face inter-action in which understandings, ideas, and opinions can be exchanged through questioning. As students think about a subject under discussion and present their views, more important learning, other than just the recall of factual information, can take place.

Plan for a discussion as completely as you would prepare for a lecture or self-paced learning activities.
The key to a successful discussion is the questions you develop and ask. Here are suggestions for formulating questions:

- Limit a question to as few words as possible.
- Treat only a single point with a question.
- Relate the question specifically to the subject being considered.
- Rarely use "closed questions" that require only a **yes** or **no** answer.
- Start with words like "why," "what," and "how" that can generate explanations, interpretations, and judgements rather than just answers consisting of facts.
- Follow-up or probe an indefinite answer with another question, requiring the student to justify, clarify, refocus, or expand an answer.

Acknowledge thoughtful answers. Encourage students to react to each other's comments and questions.

Example –

> **Sample topic:** Introduction to Digital Techniques
> **Questions:**   1. Where are digital techniques used?
>   2. Why use digital techniques?
>   3. What is the binary number system?

• Demonstration

This is teaching by showing. The purpose is to explain how a procedure or process is performed. The instructor, or other expert, explains and carries out the demonstration as students listen, watch, and ask questions. Here are suggestions to help make a demonstration successful:

- Arrange equipment and materials so everything is ready for use.
- Make certain each student can see the details of the demonstration. Sometimes the best location is over your shoulder so manipulations are observed as they would be performed. Repeat the demonstration if all students do not see it clearly the first time.
- If a student group is large, or the subject for the demonstration is small or intricate, consider setting up a video camera connected to one or more large television monitors for group viewing. By zooming in on details of the subject or the demonstration, everyone will be able to see the procedure.
- Allow for discussion and questions by students to clarify what is shown.
- Give students the opportunity to practice the skill or portions of it as the demonstration proceeds.
- Following the demonstration, plan ample time for students to refine the skill until proficiency is attained.

Refer to the use of a demonstration in on-the-job training procedure on page 153.

Example –

> **Student Group**: Photographic Technicians
> **Demonstration:** Operation of digital laser color printer

• Laboratory Activity

As previously indicated, technical training frequently involves hands-on lab work following a classroom presentation. This provides the important opportunity for students to use and practice what was learned in the classroom. Usually equipment and software products are available for use.

Here are suggestions for successful laboratory activity:

- Make certain students are prepared for the lab. Are they competent with the preparatory learning? (Successful when tested on learning objectives.)
- Distribute the manual, study guide, or worksheets, and references or job aids that direct their lab activities. Inform students as to what should be read before the lab session. Alert them to necessary safety considerations.
- Check to see that necessary equipment and materials are at hand and are operating properly.
- Provide meaningful activities, such as: set up and operate equipment, apply scientific principles, practice techniques, solve problems, simulate real situations.

- Assign students, or teams, to work stations.
- Be available for questions or for providing assistance.
- Provide sufficient time for required activities.
- Evaluate learning in realistic ways by end of session. Refer to page 62.

Example –

> **Example**: Packaging products
> **Activity**: Practice loading aerosol pressurized containers

• Simulation

This is a representation of a problem situation for a student or a team to solve. Aspects of the problem that are close to a real-life work setting are presented, often time-compressed on videotape, or a videodisc. The student may be required to perform skill manipulations, make responses, and take other actions for decision-making.

The participants have the opportunity to become deeply involved, undergoing the same stress and mental activity they would experience in reality. Some materials are sophisticated enough for students immediately to see the results of their actions or decisons.

You may have commercial materials available for use. If you wish to create your own resources to fit training needs, consider this procedure:

- Identify the learning objectives to be accomplished.
- Decide on the format for materials – real objects and equipment, video recording, or a specially constructed environment.
- Develop a scenario of the work situation including the setting, operational aspects, and responsibilities of participating students.
- Prepare materials or have them prepared.
- Write directions for students, including necessary information as preparatory background, or for use during the simulated exercise.
- Set up and tryout the training simulation.

After the activity, the instructor and students should discuss and evaluate the results, along with each person's participation.

Example –

> **Student Group**: Customer reps
> **Simulation**: Working with an upset customer to solve an equipment malfunction problem

On-the-Job Training

An important combination of both the small group (usually demonstration) and self-paced learning categories of training methods is on-the-job training (OJT). It may follow classroom instruction or be the main procedure for learning skills.

Advantages
- Instructor is a supervisor or a senior coworker.
- Training is for one individual or two – three employees.
- Training takes place in the actual work environment (shop, lab, production line, field) with same equipment as used on job.
- Skills are immediately practiced and applied.
- Learning is at a pace suitable to employee.
- Competency achieved at mastery level if procedures properly implemented.
- Content and skills taught are up-to-date and directly related to job needs.

Disadvantages
- Not a suitable method for training large number of students.
- May interfere with normal activities in workplace.
- Requires Instructor to exhibit proper attitude, and cooperative behaviors, as well as technical proficiency.

Example –

> Working with sheet metal – bending, curving annealing, and seaming.

See page 152 for details on planning and implementing on-the-job training.

Attention to Safety Guidelines

Whenever a performance skill is to be taught or practiced, care should be taken to reduce the risk of potential injury to students or other persons. It is essential to foster a safety-oriented training environment in order to avoid all preventable injuries.

Summary

1. All instructional methods fit within one of three categories: presentation to a class, self-paced learning, and group activities.

2. Selection of a training method depends on the topic's learning objectives and instructor's teaching preference.

3. For all methods of teaching and learning, refer to learning principles and practices described in Chapter 15.

4. Presentations are more appropriate for introducing and motivating an interest in a subject, for presenting essential information before individual and group activities, and for summarizing a topic.

5. Since a presentation is mostly one-way communication, it is important to provide for and encourage student participation through note-taking and answering questions.

6. Self-paced learning allows students to study at their own pace by reading, viewing media, completing worksheets, solving problems, or practicing a skill.

7. Formats for self-paced learning include: textbook/manual and worksheets, job aids, and computer-based training, as well as traditional slide/tape or audio programs.

8. Small group activities contribute to achieving affective domain objectives, learning to improve listening and speaking skills, and giving attention to problem solving and decision-making objectives.

9. Techniques of group learning include: instructor/student discussion, demonstration, lab activity, and simulation.

10. On-the-job training (OJT) is a combination of demonstration and self-paced learning for a very realistic type of training.

11. Refer to safety guidelines to avoid potential injuries to students during skill training.

Review Exercise

1. To which category of training does each situation apply?
____ a. Motivating an interest in a new topic.
____ b. Useful for servicing affective domain objectives.
____ c. Making use of a job aid.
____ d. Use a one-time guest speaker.
____ e. Best to recognize needs for students to work individually.
____ f . Simulation or demonstration is an example.

2. What two techniques can be used to encourage student participation during a lecture?

3. To which category of training does each statement apply as a NEGATIVE or UNDESIRABLE factor?
____ a. Guard against one or two students controlling the session.
____ b. Student may leave class with incorrect learning.
____ c. Requires more time for development of materials than for other training categories.
____ d. Does not satisfactorily apply the recognized principles of learning.
____ e. Requires that students be fully prepared before meeting together.
____ f . Study habits may have to be refined.

4. To which specific type of training activity does each relate?
____ a. Instructor shows video recording of operational situation and asks questions; students reply, justifying viewpoints.
____ b. Student refers to printed directions on a card while carrying out a complex procedure.
____ c. Student reads sections of a manual, completes review questions, and checks answers, while studying a topic prior to discussion in class.

___ d. To review or summarize a topic, after study activities are completed, before testing.
___ e. The overhead projector is a useful resource.
___ f . For skill learning, use as immediate follow-up of a classroom presentation.

5. When asking questions, which are good practices?
___ a. For clear, specific answers, require Yes or No replies.
___ b. Try not to use "what" or "how" words to start a question.
___ c. Follow-up a vague answer with another question.
___ d. Encourage students to react to others' answers.
___ e. Broaden a question to include reference to unrelated content beyond the subject.
___ f. Word a question briefly and directly.

Answers: 1. Presentation – a,d; Self-paced learning – c,e; Group Interaction – b,f.
2. Encourage note-taking, ask questions, students think along with instructor.
3. Presentation – b,d; Self-paced learning – c,f; Group interaction – a,e.
4. a: discussion; b: job aid for self-paced learning; c: manual/worksheet for self-paced learning; d: presentation; e: presentation; f: laboratory activity.
5. c,d,f.

References

"Analyzing and Selecting Instructional Strategies and Tactics." D. Jonassen and S. Grabinger. *Performance and Instruction Quarterly*, 1990, *3*(2), 29-47.

Classroom Questions: What Kinds? N. Sanders. New York: HarperCollins, 1966.

"Conducting Discussions." In *Instructing and Evaluating in Higher Education.* R. J. McBeath, ed. Englewood Cliffs, NJ: Educational Technology Publications, 1992.

Individualizing Instruction. R. Hiemstra and B. Sisco. San Francisco: Jossey-Bass, 1990.

Learning Through Discussion. W. Fawcett-Hall. Beverly Hills, CA: Sage, 1982.

Lecture Method of Instruction. M. M. Broadwell. Englewood Cliffs, NJ: Educational Technology Publications, 1980.

Making Instruction Work. R. F. Mager. Belmont, CA: David Lake, Publisher, 1988.

Models of Teaching. B. Joyce and M. Weil. Englewood Cliffs, NJ: Prentice-Hall, 1986.

"Preparing Lectures." In *Instructing and Evaluating in Higher Education.* R. J. McBeath, ed. Englewood Cliffs, NJ: Educational Technology Publications, 1992.

"Simulated Reality." B. Geber. *Training,* 1990, *27*(4), 41-46.

Smart Questions. D. Leeds. New York: McGraw-Hill, 1988.

Superthink: A Guide for Asking Thought-Provoking Questions. H. Davis. San Luis Obispo, CA: Dandy Lion, 1982.

Chapter 6

WHAT RESOURCES CAN I USE?

In this chapter you will learn to:

> - **Identify nine categories of training resources.**
> - **Recognize features and uses for each type of resource.**
> - **Select resources to serve specific learning objectives and content needs.**

Most successful training activities rely on the use of appropriate instructional resources. An overhead projector with transparencies may be important to the instructor who will deliver a lecture. A set of printed worksheet questions may be completed by a student as a manual is studied. Simulated episodes on videotape may be necessary with a group of students engaged in a problem-solving activity. In each instance, the resources make substantial contributions to carrying out the activities and accomplishing the objectives they were chosen to serve.

Resources should be purposefully selected to serve one or more objectives and the content for a subject or a topic. They become the channel through which you communicate information or provide other learning experiences for students. Training resources can fulfill one or more of these training purposes:

RESOURCES CAN:

1. MOTIVATE STUDENTS

2. ILLUSTRATE SUBJECT CONTENT AND PERFORMANCE SKILLS

3. PROVIDE REALISTIC LEARNING EXPERIENCES

4. HELP FORM ATTITUDES

5. PROVIDE OPPORTUNITY FOR SELF-ANALYSIS

These purposes indicate that both the efficiency of learning and a positive student attitude toward learning can be enhanced through the careful selection, preparation, and use of appropriate instructional resources.

Resources and Their Features

The resources available for training can be grouped into a number of categories. Some types are appropriate for classroom use, others are best for use by individuals, and many may have multiple uses. The most useful ones, with a brief overview of their main features, are described below. Preparation of many types of training materials is treated in the chapters of Section B of this book.

People and Real Things

- **Guest speakers** are qualified persons who can motivate as well as inform students.

- **Objects and devices** are real things that can be seen, handled, and manipulated.

Models and Mock-ups

- Substitutions can be made for real items which are too big, too small, or too complex to be made available in a classroom. **Models** are usually smaller than the original, while **mock-ups** are often larger and greatly simplified. Each permits learning an operation through careful study of the way something functions.

Printed Materials

- **Paper handouts** include outlines, diagrams, articles, worksheets, and other information on paper for reference use during a presentation or other learning activity.

- **Workbooks** contain course materials including objectives, outlines, worksheets, reprints, self-check tests, assignments, and other items for student use.

- **Textbooks or manuals** provide in-depth treatment of a subject; including chapters on course topics.

- **CD-ROMs** permit storage on small optical disc of large amounts of verbal and pictorial information that can be accessed directly.

- **Photo CDs** contain pictures recorded from film and accessed by a player or a computer equipped with a compatible drive.

- **Job aids** are prepared guides in the form of a step-by-step procedure or checklist, a list of directions, or a labelled illustration to help students correctly perform such actions as assembling, operating, or maintaining equipment. Also useful for reference use on the job.

Display Materials

- **Chalkboards and flipcharts** can display outlines, summaries, or graphics for use during group sessions.

- **Enlarged diagrams, charts, and graphs** present information and illustrations on a variety of surfaces like cardboard sheets or butcher paper.

- **Photographs** are realistic pictures of objects, situations, or procedures.

Audio Recordings

- **Audiocassette recordings** present verbal information or dramatic situations. Can serve as realistic, alternative sources of study for individuals and groups.

- **Compact discs (CD)** are commercially produced, high quality sounds, read by a laser beam.

Projected Still Pictures

- **Overhead transparencies** visualize printed and graphic information for instructor or student use in a classroom. Simple preparation methods and various visual techniques can be used for projecting information from a transparency in a lighted room.

- **Slides** are photographic reproductions of original subjects containing graphic or pictorial forms of information. Useful as projected presentations to groups and for individual study.

Projected Moving Pictures

- **Films** are considered a useful medium when motion (regular speed, slowed down, or speeded up), needs to be shown.

- **Video recordings** are preferred to film for producing motion with synchronized pictures and sound. Suitable for both group and individual uses.

Computer Technology

- **Computers** provide active learning as programs (**software**) present information, or simulate situations.

- Expressions like **computer-assisted instruction (CAI)** or **computer-based training (CBT)** are commonly used.

Combinations of Media

- **Audio recording/printed paper** combine audio narration with printed information in a verbal, graphic, or photographic form as an inexpensive, easy-to-use, self-paced learning resource.

- **Slides/audio recordings** combine narration, music, and sound effects synchronized with slides. May be shown to groups or used for individual study.

- **Interactive computer/videodisc or CD-ROM** provides sophisticated resources for classroom and individualized training as the computer controls display of information on a screen from a computer program, and from a collection of still pictures or motion sequences. Visuals may be selected in any order from connected video or compact disc source. Such **multimedia applications** can utilize the strengths of individual resources in coordinated fashion to produce very dynamic learning.

The above descriptions provide minimal information about the resources you may have available. Become familiar with each type you might use. See additional information in chapters of Section B and the use of media in Chapter 17. For further details see listed references.

Selecting Resources for Use

In many classrooms, chalkboards are installed and a flip-chart, overhead projector, video player, and other media equipment may be at hand. Also, microcomputers and other equipment may be accessible for self-instructional uses. Your choice of which resource, or combination of resources, to use should be based on the requirements of the learning objectives, the content or task to be taught, and availability of equipment.

Ask yourself questions like the following. They can guide you to suitable answers for selecting the most appropriate resources:

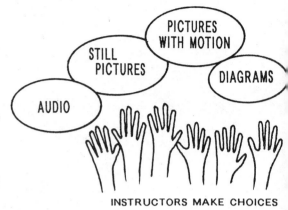

INSTRUCTORS MAKE CHOICES

- Would simple illustrations be suitable? **(chalkboard/ flipchart)**
- Should illustrations be enlarged for satisfactory viewing by the class? **(overhead transparencies)**
- Should enlarged photographs of real subjects be shown? **(slides)**
- Should motion be shown? **(video or film)**
- Should explanations or dramatic situations be described verbally? **(audio recording, with slides as necessary)**
- Should a student or a group study factual information on their own? **(text/workbook; audio recording/print; computer program, possibly including still pictures, graphics, print, and motion images)**
- Should a variable order of visuals be called up as a student studies a topic or solves a training problem? **(computer/video or other interactive format)**

By dealing with these questions, you will have some bases for deciding which type of resource should be used. You may find that a combination of types is necessary for covering a subject.

Summary

1. Resources for training can be grouped into eight categories: real things, print, displays, audio recordings, projected still pictures, projected motion pictures, computer technology, and combinations of media.

2. When resources are being selected for use, questions relating to requirements of learning objectives and content, as well as availability of equipment, can lead to satisfactory choices.

Review Exercise

1. For which reasons would media be used in training?
___ a. To illustrate content.
___ b. To expose students to more realistic explanation than only a verbal presentation.
___ c. To fill class time after regular work is finished.
___ d. To replace employment of an expert.

___ e. To motivate an interest in the subject.

___ f . To influence an attitude.

2. To which type of training resource does each statement relate?

___ a. Illustrating a procedure requiring physical movement.

___ b. Having an expert talk to a class.

___ c. Using a small replica of a piece of complex equipment.

___ d. Showing a small group of students diagrams and summaries as you make a presentation.

___ e. Using realistic pictures of detailed subjects for viewing in a large class.

___ f . Providing for active student participation while using still and moving picture sequences viewed in various arrangements.

___ g. Showing a large class diagrams and printed lists as part of a lecture.

3. What four factors should be examined when deciding which media to select for training?

Answers: 1. a,b,e,f.

         2. a – video; b – real person; c – model; d – flipchart or chalkboard; e – slides; f – interactive computer/video; g – overhead transparencies.

         3. Learning objectives, subject content or skill task, equipment available, students and their learning styles.

References

The ASTD Handbook of Instructional Technology. G.M. Piskurich, ed. New York: McGraw-Hill, 1993.

Directory of Multimedia Equipment, Software & Services and Video, Computer & Audio-Visual Products. International Communication Industries Association. Fairfax, VA. (annual publications).

Instructional Media and the New Technologies of Instruction. R. Heinich and others. New York: Macmillan, 1993.

Planning, Producing, and Using Instructional Technologies. J. E. Kemp and D. C. Smellie. New York: HarperCollins, 1993.

Selecting and Developing Media for Instruction. A. Reynolds and R. H. Anderson. Cincinnati, OH: Van Nostrand Reinhold, 1992.

Selecting Media for Instruction. R. A. Reiser and R. M. Gagne. Englewood Cliffs, NJ: Educational Technology Publications, 1983.

Visual Communicating. R. E. Wileman. Englewood Cliffs, NJ: Educational Technology Publications, 1993.

Visual Information. R. Pettersson. Englewood Cliffs, NJ: Educational Technology Publications, 1993.

Chapter **7**

HOW DO I TEST STUDENT LEARNING?

In this chapter you will learn to:

- **Recognize the importance of competency-based standards in training programs.**
- **Relate test questions to learning objectives.**
- **Prepare four types of test questions to measure cognitive objectives.**
- **Prepare tests and two evaluation forms to measure psychomotor objectives.**
- **Recognize the use of two instruments for judging changes in affective behavior to evaluate attitudes and interpersonal relations.**

Now comes the time to determine SUCCESS — your students' success in learning and your success in teaching. How well each student attains what your learning objectives require, must be determined by some type of testing or other evaluation.

Standards of Achievement

In a successful training program, as many students as possible should attain a satisfactory level of achievement specified as the standard of performance in your learning objectives. The terms **competency-based training** or **mastery learning** apply to a program in which each student reaches the required level of comprehension and competence.

If a student does not attain the level of preset competence after being tested, arrangements can be made for the student to review the information or further practice the skill. Another form of the test, containing different wording but similar meaning questions to measure attainment of objectives, or the same performance evaluation, can give the student another opportunity to demonstrate mastery.

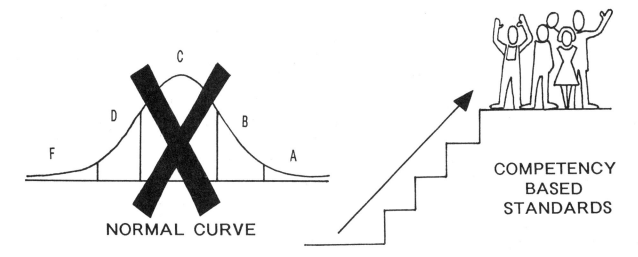

NORMAL CURVE

COMPETENCY BASED STANDARDS

This competency-based procedure differs from the traditional academic method of grading students on a **normal curve**. In the latter procedure, students receive a letter mark of **A-B-C-D-F**. Each student is compared with all others in the class. The final grade is a **relative** measure of capability only within the group. This "norm-referenced" measure tells the instructor that one student is more proficient than another student, but not much information about the degree of proficiency with respect to the knowledge and tasks that were learned.

The **competency-based** method (represented by the "**A**" grade for the great majority, if not all, students in a class), as advocated in this book, should be applied. (Would you accept an operation by a surgeon who was graded "C" on treating appendicitis?)

Relation Between Testing and Learning Objectives

Some instructors find it difficult to prepare a test. They struggle to think up questions relating to the content they have taught. This is a difficult way to go. You do not "think up" questions. The learning objectives can help direct you to the test questions.

The **verb** used in an objective indicates the form that a test item should take. Here are some examples:

> • To **identify** or **recognize**:
>   Choosing an answer in an objective-type item
> • To **list** or **label**:
>   Writing a word or a brief statement
> • To **state** or **describe**:
>   Writing a short or lengthy answer
> • To **solve** or **calculate**:
>   Writing or choosing a solution or numerical answer
> • To **formulate** or **organize**:
>   Writing a plan or choosing an order of items relative to a plan
> • To **operate** or **use**:
>   Rating the quality of performance against criteria

The above examples illustrate the close relationship that is necessary between a **learning objective** and its **test item**. The verb in an objective guides the students' study and then alerts them how to prepare for the test. Often the expression **criterion-referenced instruction** is used to represent this close relationship.

Testing Cognitive (Knowledge) Objectives

Most cognitive-domain objectives (see page 24) are evaluated by paper and pencil tests. These are grouped into two categories – **objective** questions or **written-answer** forms.

Objective Questions This category includes questions for which the student must recognize and select an answer from two or more choices, or respond to prepared statements. No writing, other than marking an answer, is required. There are two commonly-used types of objective tests — **multiple choice** and **true/false**.

A **multiple choice item** consists of a **stem** which is a question, a problem, or an incomplete statement. The possible answers are called **options** or **alternatives**.

They may number from three to five, with only one of them being the correct or best reply.

By carefully stating the stem and selecting reasonable options, both recall of information and more complex objectives in the cognitive domain can be tested with multiple choice questions. Guessing is reduced because there are three to five potential answers from which to choose (as compared to the 50% chance of guessing the correct answer in a true/false question).

When developing multiple choice test items, plan for:

- clear wording of the stem so it cannot be misinterpreted by the student;
- emphasizing a special word in the stem to call attention to it by capitalizing or underlining (examples: NOT or least important);
- using three to five answer options from which selection can be made;
- making certain all responses are reasonable, although only one is correct;
- placing correct answers in a random order through the test (for example, not having the third alternative as the correct one in most items on a test).

Here are examples of multiple choice test items:

Recall level:
As used in a numerical control document, which term is the proper condition of having all elements of a surface in one plane?
   a. straightness
   b. parallelism
   c. profile of a surface
   d. flatness
   e. runout

Higher level:
Refer to the print of Angle Plate D-1. The distance between the zero point and hole #4 on the Y axis is:
   a. .250"   c. 1.469"
   b. .531"   d. 1.625"

A **True/False item** presents a statement for replies like **"true-false," "yes-no," "fact-opinion,"** or **"agree-disagree."** The elements of content that can be tested are fairly narrow, often being limited to the recall of factual information.

Here are examples of true/false test items:

True/False: Serial data transmission is faster than parallel data transmission.

Fact/Opinion: For cabinet construction, Ponderosa pine is preferable to Douglas fir for use.

A variation of the usual true/false question is to require the student to add a word or phrase to correct a false statement. This can reduce guessing, since the student must know why the statement is false.

Here are examples of this true/false variation:

> **True/False**: *Evaporation* is the change of water from a vapor to a liquid state.
> (Answer: False – *Condensation*)
>
> If the statement is False, describe what would make it True.
> An LP gas burner flame is properly adjusted when the flame has a yellow tip.
> (Answer: False – a *blue-green* inner flame with no yellow in the flame)

Because they seem easy to write, true/false items are very popular. Unless thought and care are given to be certain that the statement is entirely true or entirely false, students can misinterpret the intended meaning. This can lead to confusion and potential disagreements.

Written Answer Questions

The major limitation of the above objective-type items is that students are not required to plan answers or express themselves in their own words. These shortcomings are overcome by using written answer questions. They may range from the requirements of a one-word response to a lengthy reply (a paragraph, a page, or an essay).

A **short answer item** requires the students to complete a statement or answer a question with a single word, numbers, phrase, or sentence.

Here are examples of short answer test items:

> 1. A maximum of _____ conductors are permitted in wireways and having a _____ % of fill.
>
> 2. What is the resistance of a 500 foot line of #10 copper cable? (Refer to Table 8.)

An **essay item** is most useful for requiring the student to organize and express thoughts in a logical way. An answer may require the analysis of a situation, or explaining actions to solve a problem.

Here is an example of an essay test item:

> When using an ammeter, what precautions need to be taken?

Because essay test items seem easy to write, questions can be ambiguous, making scoring difficult. Therefore, when preparing to evaluate an essay test, you should set criteria for deciding on the number of points or the grade to be given for each answer. Do this by preparing an acceptable answer yourself, based on the objective and subject content. Make a list of the facts, concepts, or other information that should be treated in the answer. Then assign numerical values to the main points.

Here is an example:

> **Objective**: To write a description of the process that air and fuel undergo when a diesel engine cylinder is equipped with a precombustion chamber.
>
> **Test Question**: Explain what happens to air and fuel oil when a precombustion chamber is added to a diesel engine cylinder.
>
> **Key Points for Acceptable Answer:**   Numerical Value
> 1. Air compressed and forced through narrow neck   2
> 2. Friction causes higher temperature   2
> 3. Ignited fuel entering chamber increases pressure,
>   forcing mixture into cylinder   4
> 4. Uniform combustion and pressure in cylinder   3

Because of the requirements of the learning objectives, a test on a topic may consist of a combination of both objective and written answer questions. In developing them, carefully plan format and wording. Direct student thinking to the acceptable answer by careful phrasing. For further help with formulating properly stated questions, see the references for this chapter.

If a training course will be conducted frequently, it would be desirable to develop a collection of test items for topic objectives. Then random selection can be made so the same objectives are tested, using different test items. By having a number of questions for each learning objective, you can be more certain that incoming students are not informed of test questions by former students. It does happen! Computer software packages can guide you to create a bank of test items.

Testing Psychomotor (Skill) Objectives

By using a performance test you are able to determine how well a student can carry-out a particular skill. Attention has already been given to the means for evaluating cognitive knowledge required for a skill (identifying equipment parts, their functions, and so on), with objective test items. Now the level of skill competency needs to be determined.

The kinds of learning that can be evaluated, as related to psychomotor behavior, include:

- **Physical skills** – using machines and tools, operating procedures, doing construction and repair work.
- **Mental skills** – trouble-shooting, problem solving behavior, human relations skills.
- **End result product** – appearance and/or operation of item constructed, prepared, installed, and repaired; also quantity of items produced.

Develop the Test

Once you have reviewed the objectives for the test and details of the skill, follow this procedure for designing the test:

1. Write down the steps or specific procedures of the skill that should comprise the performance to be judged. Establish the proficiency level

that will be accepted (as indicated in the performance standard of the learning objective).

2. Plan whether the testing performance should be under simulated or realistic conditions, in the classroom, laboratory, or at the worksite.
3. List the equipment, materials, and printed resources to be available to students during testing.
4. Decide on the amount of time needed to test a student.
5. Consider any precautions that should be taken for safety.
6. Write instructions that direct the actions of students during the test.
7. Inform any persons, other than students (helpers, evaluators), about their responsibilities during the test.
8. As necessary, advise other appropriate individuals (supervisors, coworkers) that a testing procedure will be in effect (location and time) so as not to interfere with normal activities.

Design Skill Measurement Form

When evaluating a skill, the instructor or other qualified person, observes student actions and rates the performance. The ratings are commonly made by using a checklist.

The **checklist** determines whether sequential steps or other actions are successfully performed. The evaluator places a check mark for each item or indicates a **"yes-no"** or **"done-not done."** The form also can be used to assess quality of performance by indicating "satisfactory" or "unsatisfactory" for each step.

Example of a checklist:

```
┌─────────────────────────────────────────────────────────────────────┐
│  Objective: Joining sections of PVC plastic pipe                      │
│                                                                       │
│  OK   Not OK          Action                     Criteria             │
│  ____  ____   1. Check ends of pipe        Burr or sharp edge found   │
│  ____  ____   2. Remove burr or sharp edge                            │
│  ____  ____   3. Sand and clean surfaces    Use clean cloth           │
│  ____  ____   4. Apply primer               Enough, not excess, dry   │
│  ____  ____   5. Apply cement to pipe       Liberally, surface more that│
│                                             socket depth              │
│  ____  ____   6. Apply cement to socket     Lightly, completely       │
│                  surface                                              │
│  ____  ____   7. Insert pipe into socket    Immediately, full socket  │
│                                             depth, rotate 1/4 turn    │
│  ____  ____   8. Hold joint together        Minimum 15 seconds        │
│  ____  ____   9. Wipe off excess cement                               │
└─────────────────────────────────────────────────────────────────────┘
```

Design Product Quality Form

A **rating scale** can be used to judge the quality (and quantity) of a resulting product. A numerical scale with descriptive criteria is commonly used. It consists of standards from low (1) to high (3 to 5).

Such factors as these may be included:

- General appearance of product.
- Accuracy of product details (shape, dimensions, fit, finish).
- Relation among components or parts (size, fit, finish, color).
- Workability (operation, sound, movement).
- Quantity of acceptable products produced during a time period.

Example of Product Rating Scale:

Objective: To make 8"x10" color prints from 35mm color negatives

Criteria: focus, framing, true colors, color saturation

Unacceptable: 1 or more criteria show – poor focus, framing off, colors not true, colors washed out or too dense

Acceptable: Some slight shifts in criteria between unacceptable and superior

Superior: Criteria show sharp focus, tasteful and accurate framing, colors true, full color saturation

(1)	(2)	(3)	(4)	(5)
Unacceptable		Acceptable		Superior

An important limitation for using rating scales can be any personal bias an evaluator may have in giving preference to one student over another for any of a number of reasons. Also, careful attention is required to discriminate each level from the others on a scale.

Prior to Using the Test

Before the test is to be used, it should be tried out with a sampling of two or three persons from the potential training group or equivalent individuals. This trial allows checking for:

- the person's clear understanding of the testing procedure;
- the effectiveness of each part of the test;
- the required length of the testing period for each person.

If more than a single person will serve as evaluator, the procedure should be standardized so that each individual making a judgement would grade a similar performance equally. Have the evaluators rate samples of products and then discuss their decisions to reach consensus.

Evaluating Affective (Attitudinal) Objectives

You probably found that writing attitudinal and interpersonal objectives was a challenging task. Now to evaluate them is equally demanding. The feelings, values, beliefs, and personal behaviors of individuals are very private matters that cannot be measured easily. (Review page 27, with special attention to the list of cues for successful attitude change.)

The problems of evaluating these objectives is further compounded because the results may not become evident until sometime after training is completed. Therefore, at some appropriate time, like three months after the course is concluded, request that the immediate supervisors of former students complete an attitudinal evaluation form that you provide for them. The data gathered can indicate how attitudes, in terms of the affective objectives in the course, are now being met.

When evaluating changes in attitude, sometimes more than a supervisor's rating may be needed. Consider opinions expressed by the following:

- Other employees with whom the individual works.
- The customer or public being served.
- Any records filed with a complaint department within the organization.
- Quality control service for production.

Two evaluation instruments are commonly used for judging attitude changes.

Questionnaire

A series of questions can be asked for which the supervisor writes brief answers to describe the individual's behavior as representative of an attitude.

Here is an example of an attitudinal questionnaire:

> **Topic**: Automated Package Operation (see example, page 149)
>
> How well does the technician –
> 1. Use correct procedures and follow safety regulations?
> 2. Respond to unforeseen problems and emergencies?
> 3. Keep up with new developments relating to the job?
> 4. Maintain required records?
> 5. Conserve materials and maintain a neat work area?
> 6. Share technical information with other employees?

Rating Scale

A number of behaviors for a topic are listed that relate to the affective objectives in the training course. After observing the former student's performance, the supervisor rates each item as YES/NO or on a numerical scale.

Here is an example of a rating scale for attitudes:

> 1. Follows correct procedures and safety regulations
>
> Unsatisfactory   Acceptable   Superior
>
> 2. Responds to unforeseen problems and emergencies
>
> Very slow   Acceptable   Promptly
>
> 3. Keeps up with new developments relating to job
>
> Poorly   Acceptable   Very well

Summary

1. Training should be designed so that as many students as possible reach satisfactory levels of achievement. This is known as competency-based training or mastery learning.

2. The expression criterion-referenced instruction represents the close relationship between objectives and test items.

3. The verb used in a learning objective indicates the form of a test item.

4. Cognitive objectives can be tested by either objective-type or written-answer questions.

5. Objective questions are either of multiple choice or true/false form.

6. Written answer questions are of short answer or essay form.

7. Grade an essay test by preparing an acceptable answer listing the essential points for inclusion, and giving them point values.

8. A test for a psychomotor objective determines how well the student can perform a skill.

9. In developing a performance test, refer specifically to eight items: (a) procedure of the skill, (b) where testing will take place, (c) equipment and materials needed, (d) testing time, (e) instructions to students, (f) precautions for safety, (g) informing other persons who will help, and (h) advising other appropriate individuals that testing will take place.

10. The measuring instruments for a performance test can be either a checklist or a rating scale.

11. Before using a psychomotor test, try it out with two or three persons.

12. Evaluate accomplishment of affective objectives, sometime after completion of training, with a questionnaire, rating scale, or review of employee records.

Review Exercise

1. Which items are TRUE as related to testing of learning?
___ a. Among the forms of objective tests, the multiple choice is the better type to measure higher level objectives.
___ b. Essay tests are both easier to write and to grade than are objective tests.
___ c. Questions requiring the writing of numerical answers are classed as objective tests.
___ d. A major limitation of true/false items is the high possibility of correctly guessing an answer.
___ e. Performance tests are designed primarily to measure physical skills.
___ f . Bias may come into play during testing a performance.

___ g. It is possible to simulate a performance and judge it as if it was a real situation.
___ h. Students are graded A-B-C-D-F in a competency-based training program.
___ i . A rating scale differs from a checklist in that the former includes a number of levels for judging each component of a skill while the latter does not have any levels.

2. What is an appropriate test question or testing procedure for each learning objective?
    a. To describe the difference between *radial* and *extended-plenum* duct systems used for warm-air distribution within a heating system.

    b. To select adhesive material appropriate for securing various types of plastic to metal.

    c. To develop a teaching program for robotic welding.

3. What method of paper and pencil testing would you select for each of the following?
___ a. To supply the key word(s) for completing a sentence.
___ b. To organize information and express oneself in some detail.
___ c. To respond to a statement in an "either-or" fashion.
___ d. To select a phrase, from a number of options, that correctly answers a question or completes a statement.
___ e. To judge a performance by making sure that all steps in the procedure have been completed in proper order.

4. Which items are good practice when developing test items?
___ a. Capitalize special words in the stem of a multiple choice item.
___ b. Include unrelated responses in a multiple choice item to distract students.
___ c. A true/false item can be partly true to make students think more.
___ d. For a true/false item, it is possible to require other than just a true/false reply.
___ e. For completing a short answer item, a single word, number, phrase, or complete sentence may be required.
___ f . A vaguely worded essay question will require more thought by the student, thus making the scoring easier.
___ g. Prepare the ideal answer for an essay question and give numerical value to each component of information.

Answers: 1. a,d,e,f,g,i.
    2. (Possible answers ... there can be other ones.)
    a. Explain how two heating system installations differ with respect to physical differences and costs: (1) a radial duct system, (2) an extended-plenum duct system.
    b. (Multiple choice question) – Which kind of adhesive would you use for each situation?
    (1) Repairing china and glass objects. (answer – epoxy)
    (2) Repairing boat sails and canvas tents. (answer – acrylonitrile)
    (3) Adhering wood or metal parts together for outdoor use. (answer – acrylic)
    c. List the elements to include in instruction and specify details at each step.
    3. a. short answer; b. essay; c. true/false; d. multiple choice; e. checklist.
    4. a,d,e,g.

References

"Analyzing Knowledge-Based Tests." R.L. Sullivan and others. *Technical and Skills Training.* 1993, *4* (1), 13-18.

"Constructing Multiple Choice Test Items"
"Constructing and Scoring Essay Questions"
"Constructing True/False Test Items"
"Item Analysis on Objective Tests"
"Performance Testing"
    All above In *Instructing and Evaluating in Higher Education.* R. J. McBeath, ed. Englewood Cliffs, NJ: Educational Technology Publications, 1992.

Criterion-Referenced Test Development. S. A. Schrock and W. C. Coscarelli. Reading, MA: Addison-Wesley, 1989.

Evaluation to Improve Learning. B. S. Bloom and others. New York: McGraw-Hill, 1981.

How to Construct Achievement Tests. N .E. Gronlund. Englewood Cliffs, NJ: Prentice-Hall, 1987.

How to Measure Attitudes. M. Henerson, L. Morris, and C. Fitz-Gibbon. Newbury Park, CA: Sage Publications, 1987.

How to Measure Performance and Use Tests. L. Morris, C. Fitz-Gibbon, and E. Lindheim. Newbury Park, CA: Sage Publications, 1987.

Measuring Instructional Intent. R. F. Mager. Belmont, CA: Fearon/Pitman, 1986.

Performance Assessment in Education and Training: Alternative Techniques. M. Priestley. Englewood Cliffs, NJ: Educational Technology Publications, 1982.

Test Construction for Training Evaluation. C. Denova. New York: Van Nostrand Reinhold, 1982.

Section B

PREPARING INSTRUCTIONAL MATERIALS

As an instructor, you will discover the need to make use of various types of media to help you communicate your subject content effectively. As you learned in Chapter 6, there are many resources to consider for use in training. Various commercially prepared materials like video recordings, and computer software may be available to you. You should make selections based on instructional needs which relate to your stated learning objectives and subject content for each topic.

Useful commercial materials, especially for teaching basic skills in technical areas (electronics, construction, machine technology, and so forth) are available. Check resources within your organization, through local library or media services, or as reported in journals serving your technical area. The following catalogs (and other ones) may be found in many library reference sections:

- *CD-ROM Directory*
    Detroit, MI: Omnigraphics, Inc.
- *Educational Film and Video Locator*
    New York: R. R. Bowker
- *Indices to Educational Media* (including Vocation and Technical Audiovisuals)
    Albuquerque, NM: National Information Center for Educational Media
- *The Educational Software Locator*
    Seattle, WA: The Educational Software Center
- *Videodisc Compendium*
    St. Paul, MN: Emerging Technology Consultants, Inc.

Commercially produced materials often are designed to reach a wide range of audiences and may not be specific enough for your needs. At that point, consideration should be given to planning and preparing your own materials. The procedure follows a step-by-step path which is similar for all forms of media:

1. Identify need for media preparation (page 51)
    (What media need to be prepared for each topic?)
2. Recognize characteristics of class members (Chapter 3)
    (Are they entry level or experienced?)
3. Establish objectives (Chapter 4)
    (What should students know or be able to do as a result of media use?)
4. Decide on content (Chapter 2)
    (What will be included in each material?)
5. Confirm media selection (page 54)
    (What type(s) – print, overhead transparencies, slides, video ...?)
6. Prepare media (Chapters 8-14)
    (What procedure should be followed?)
7. Use the media for instruction (Chapter 17)
    (What plan is necessary for using each type of media?)
8. Evaluate use (Chapters 7 and 18)
    (Did the materials accomplish what you intended?)

This section covers essential information for making and using the following instructor-prepared materials:

Chapter **8. Chalkboards and Flipcharts**
Chapter **9. Printed Materials**
Chapter **10. Overhead Transparencies**
Chapter **11. Slides and Slide/Tape Programs**
Chapter **12. Audio Recordings**
Chapter **13. Video Recordings**
Chapter **14. Interactive Technologies**

Chapter **8**

CHALKBOARDS and FLIPCHARTS

In this chapter you will learn how to:

> • **Recognize the features of chalkboards and flipcharts which make them useful in training.**
> • **Plan and prepare materials for the chalkboard.**
> • **Plan and prepare materials for the flipchart.**
> • **Use chalkboards and flipcharts in training.**

Among the simplest types of instructional media are the chalkboard and the flipchart. They are easy to use as an instructor makes a presentation.

The Chalkboard

Almost every training center has some kind of chalkboard available for use. It could be one of the traditional blackboards, a type available in a variety of colors, or even one of the newer white boards which require special colored markers in place of chalk.

Features

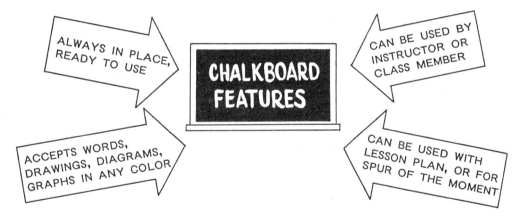

ALWAYS IN PLACE, READY TO USE

CHALKBOARD FEATURES

CAN BE USED BY INSTRUCTOR OR CLASS MEMBER

ACCEPTS WORDS, DRAWINGS, DIAGRAMS, GRAPHS IN ANY COLOR

CAN BE USED WITH LESSON PLAN, OR FOR SPUR OF THE MOMENT

Planning
• Even though the chalkboard fills the need for spontaneous use, with a little preplanning it can become an even more effective instructional tool. Decide ahead of time what will be put on the board. Plan to list key words, phrases, short sentences, or to draw simple illustrations.

• Decide how you will arrange the information on the board so it will be clearly understood and easily followed by students.

Preparing
• All chalkboard lettering should be large enough for every class member to see. Lettering that is 3 to 5 inches high would be adequate for the average 35 foot classroom. To be certain, check this prior to the class meeting. Write a line of lettering on the chalkboard and go to the back of the room to see if it can easily be read.

- It is a good idea to PRINT the lettering on the board. This generally is easier to read than is manuscript writing. Capital letters are suitable for most wording. Avoid the mistake of using capital and lower case letters in the same word or sentence as this is counter to the accepted rules of capitalization.

A BASIC ALPHABET OF CAPITAL LETTERS SUITABLE FOR
CHALKBOARDS, FLIPCHARTS, AND OTHER GRAPHIC MATERIALS

ABCDEFGHIJKLMNOP
QRSTUVWXYZ

DO NOT MIX ROMAN AND GOTHIC LETTERING TOGETHER.
ROMAN LETTERS HAVE SERIFS, WHILE GOTHIC LETTERS DO NOT.

SERIFS R ROMAN   **G** GOTHIC

- If charts, illustrations, or diagrams are to be prepared, and drawing them on the chalkboard is difficult, prepare the original on nothing larger than 8 1/2 x 11 inch paper, or use an available prepared drawing. Place the sheet in an opaque projector. Project the image onto the board surface and trace it with chalk or a chalkboard pen.

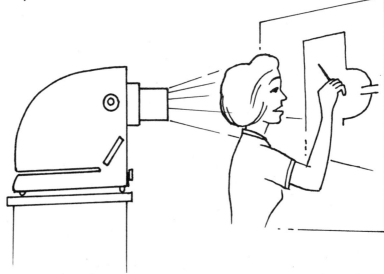

- Many of the newer chalkboards and whiteboards are metal-based. This gives the instructor the option of placing pictures, photographs, strips of lettering, or other prepared materials on the board surface with magnets holding them in place. Magnets, in the form of adhesive-backed rubberized strips, can be cut to size and attached to the back of material to be displayed.

- When selecting chalk, whether white or colored, pick the kind specifically made for chalkboard use. Some types of chalk are not suitable, such as those made for marking on surfaces like wood or metal. Such chalk will not only damage the board surface, but also will be hard to remove.

- When writing on whiteboard surfaces, it is important to use only the felt pens labelled for these surfaces. If a mistake is made and the wrong felt pen is used, the mark can be removed in two ways:

  1. Go over all lines with the proper kind of felt pen; then erase the marks.
  2. Erase the lines using the liquid material made for cleaning the magnetic heads of a videocassette recorder.

Using the Chalkboard

- Most chalkboards are located at the front of a classroom, usually behind the instructor when facing the class. This results in the instructor having to turn away from the class to use the board. Overcome this by turning back to face the class every so often. Do not talk to the chalkboard.

- Avoid standing in front of the material you have just written. Step to one side so that what is on the chalkboard can be seen.

- Be neat! The chalkboard should not be considered as a gigantic doodle pad!

- Try to put the lines of lettering on the board without going uphill or downhill. To assist in doing this, place a few level dots across the board to aim at while lettering. If the first line of lettering can be put on evenly, all that follows will be level.

- Consider placing material on the board ahead of time. Cover the writing with a pull-down projection screen. Raise the screen when you are ready to present the material to the class. It will avoid the necessity to turn away and face the board. This procedure will also save time.

- Occasionally step away from the front of the room and move out among the students. This gives you the opportunity to look at what they are seeing. Judge the legibility and clarity of material on the chalkboard.

- Once the presentation has been completed, and the class has made notes, erase the material so that it will not distract from what you may do next.

The Flipchart

The flipchart, like the chalkboard, represents a simple tool for communicating effectively. Although the flipchart can be used spontaneously in the classroom, a better plan would be to prepare the pages ahead of time. Some pages may be partially developed to be completed as a presentation is made.

As with the chalkboard, the flipchart can be used to display both verbal and graphic information:

- verbal information includes: words, lists, labels, statements
- graphic information includes: diagrams, sketches, detailed illustrations, graphs

Features

Regular flipchart paper, which measures 27 by 34 inches, comes as a pad with two kinds of sheets, blank with no marks, or with light blue lines that serve as guides for lettering. The blue-lined page has both horizontal and vertical lines which are not easily seen by the seated students.

A new "static image" flipchart material offers two important advantages. First, because the material consists of plastic sheets, it can be written on with felt pen markers. By using **waterbased** pens, the marks may be easily erased. Second, the pages can be separated from the pad and placed against a wall or other surface to which they will cling.

Planning and Preparing

- Flipcharts should be planned for viewing by a group approximately no larger than 30 to 35 in number. With larger classes, put the same information on transparencies for use with the overhead projector from front of the class.

- As with the chalkboard, simple, capital letters should be used for maximum legibility. They should be about two inches in height.

- List only key words or phrases. Limit material to five or six words per line and six or seven lines per sheet.

- The use of a light blue pencil will help to plan where to put lettering and drawings on a sheet. Draw over the blue lines with felt pens.

- When selecting writing tools, both felt pens and crayons can be used. Broad-tipped felt pens are preferable to fine-tipped pens for better legibility. Waterbased felt pens will not soak through to the next page, while felt pens with permanent ink will do so. Check the label on the pen!

- If permanent felt pens are to be used, it is a good idea to place a blank sheet temporarily between the flipchart sheets to protect the second page.

- Many felt pens appear to "dry out" before the ink is used up. This occurs because the cap has been left off for long periods of time, causing the felt tip to become dry and restrict the flow of ink. A good rule to follow is to tightly cap a felt pen when not in use. Before discarding a felt pen, try "rejuvenating" it so that the "locked in" ink supply will flow again.   To accomplish this, do the following:

Waterbased pens: Dip the tip of the pen in water until the pen soaks up enough water to release the ink supply.
Permanent ink pens: Soak the tip of the pen in denatured alcohol (non-water alcohol) to release the ink supply.

For both types of pens, this procedure should only take a few minutes.

•To place illustrations, charts, or diagrams onto a flipchart page, project an image of the original by using the opaque projector as described previously; then trace the graphic form.

Using the Flipchart

• Stand beside the flipchart, not in front of it. Talk to the class and not to the chart.

• If the instructor asks students to read material on a flipchart page, give them time to do so. It is frustrating to start discussing new content while individuals are still reading the previous material.

• Just as with the chalkboard, the instructor should occasionally look at the flipchart from the point of view of the students. Move around the room and view the display. Is it easily seen from the back of the room?

• It is possible to place lightly penciled notes along the edge of the paper. The instructor can see them and use them as reference. They would not be visible to the class.   Without having to hold a sheet of notes, the instructor can make a smoother presentation.

• If further reference needs to be made to a page already shown, tear it from the pad and tape it to a wall surface. In the case of "static-image" paper, as stated previously, the sheet will adhere to the wall without tape.

Summary

1. The chalkboard and flipchart are among the simplest types of instructional media for classroom use.

2. Material to be presented should be planned so information is well organized and legible to students.

3. Felt pens are available in both waterbased and permanent types, each one having special features.

4. An instructor should be positioned so as not to talk to the board or chart, nor to block out what has been written on either surface.

Review Exercise

1. Which statements are TRUE about the chalkboard?
___ a. Lettering about one inch tall is suitable for most uses.
___ b. It is better to avoid mixing upper and lower case lettering in the same word.
___ c. White surface chalkboards require the use of special felt pens.
___ d. Any colored chalk can be used on a chalkboard.
___ e. You can attach illustrations with magnets to some chalkboards.
___ f. As you write on the chalkboard, you should turn to the class when speaking.

2. Which statements are TRUE about flipcharts?
___ a. Without much practice, it is difficult to print letters even and straight on flipchart paper.
___ b. When using a permanent felt pen, protect adjacent sheets on which you will write by placing a blank sheet of paper behind the sheet on which you write.
___ c. Limit lettering to 10 lines on a flipchart sheet.
___ d. A fine-tipped felt pen is best for lettering and ease of reading.
___ e. The best way to determine if you have a waterbased or permanent felt pen is to check the label.

3. Describe how you might handle each situation:
   a. When writing on the chalkboard, your lines of lettering, across the board, run downhill.

   b. You have drawn a diagram on the chalkboard before class, but you do not want to show it until you are ready to use it.

   c. You have a relatively new waterbased felt pen that does not make continuous color lines and the tip feels hard.

   d. You have prepared a number of flipchart pages before class. You will tear each one off and adhere it on the wall after you refer to it. But you do not want to have the next sheet seen, on the flipchart, until you are ready to refer to it.

_____

Answers: 1. b,c,e,f.
         2. b,e.
         3. a. Place a few dots straight across the board to guide the first line.
            b. Cover it with a pull-down projection screen or stand a portable screen in front of the board.
            c. Soak the tip in water and rub it on paper.
            d. Leave a blank sheet between each sheet on which something is written. Pull off each blank when ready to show the sheet underneath.

References

Chalk Talks. C. E. Schwarz. Springfield, IL: Charles C. Thomas Publishing, 1986.

Flip Charts: How To Draw and How to Use Them. R. C. Brandt. Richmond, VA: Brandt Management Group, 1987.

Planning, Producing, and Using Instructional Technologies. J. E. Kemp and D. C. Smellie. New York: HarperCollins, 1993.

Successful Flipcharts: How to Make and Use Them. G. W. Cochern. San Jose, CA: Instructional Media Productions, 1989.

Chapter **9**

PRINTED MATERIALS

In this chapter you will learn to:

- **Recognize those features of printed materials that make them useful in training.**
- **Plan and prepare printed materials, including words and illustrations.**
- **Use printed materials in training.**

As an instructor, you expect your students to organize the material you present in class by taking notes. This gives them a record of what was covered so that it can be reviewed and used at a later time. While this is a common practice, it does not always work satisfactorily.

Unfortunately, many students may not always take good notes, while others may not be clear about what you said. Therefore, their notes are not totally accurate. To help overcome these problems, develop printed materials that can be distributed to your class so students have correct information they can take with them. These handouts can accompany the instructor's use of transparencies, chalkboard, and flipchart materials.

Everyone is familiar with printed materials. If you develop items for use in your teaching, you need to refer first to the selection of content, then to writing, editing, and preparation methods.

Features

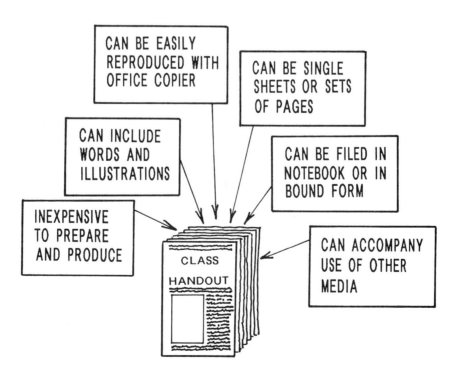

Types of Printed Materials

The following kinds of printed materials often are prepared for use by students in training programs:

- An outline or summary for a lesson.
- A worksheet, including questions or statements with space for answers or notes.
- A list of new terms with definitions.
- A procedure described in step-by-step order or directions for training activities (a job aid).
- One or more illustrations or detailed diagrams with labels (a job aid).
- Copies of information from flipcharts or transparencies.
- A complete study guide or manual for a topic.

If pages of printed information (including copyrighted articles from journals or other sources) are to be reproduced and distributed, then **permission to reproduce** should be obtained from the copyright holder as indicated in the publication.

Planning and Preparing Printed Materials

As with other kinds of resources, planning and preparing printed materials from a single page to a complete publication requires consideration of:

- Learning objectives to be accomplished.
- Level of student understanding of vocabulary to be used.
- Competence with word processing software.
- Assistance needed (secretarial, artwork, photography).

Word Selection

- Use simple, easily understood words unless technical terms are required, explaining the latter as they are introduced.
- Be consistent in capitalizing words and in abbreviating expressions.
- Emphasize words, phrases, or sentences with CAPITALIZED, underlined, **boldfaced**, or *italicized* words.
- Keep paragraphs short because lengthy paragraphs discourage careful reading.
- Plan to use headings and subheads to identify separate sections of a topic.
- For a multi-page guide or manual, develop an outline or a table of contents to help class members locate information.

Illustrations

Pictures, diagrams, and other illustrations help in understanding the written words. They support the retention of the information. Their use can be to:

- clarify information treated in words;
- illustrate equipment parts, functions, and names;
- show how a procedure is carried out;
- substitute for a lengthy verbal explanation;
- make printed material attractive.

The preparation of illustrations can be:

- drawn by hand;
- created from a graphics software program and "imported" to its position with a desktop computer program;
- scanned into computer memory from an original, and then imported.

The use of photographs and color pictures requires more complex duplication procedures or reproduction with a color printer.

Combining Words and Illustrations

Decide on the page design. This might be only a title, followed by a list of items. In other situations, the page could include typed material along with illustrations. Place an illustration close to the words associated with it. If an illustration is either too small or too large for use, it can be enlarged or reduced by many office photocopy machines.

After selecting the proper size illustrations and preparing the typed information, all parts can be fastened to a page with an adhesive material. This page becomes the **master** from which the needed number of copies can be reproduced for class use. Number all pages consecutively.

A personal computer, with appropriate software, can be used to convert rough copy you write into final form. With a **desktop publishing** program, pages can be designed with blank space for illustrations to be added. Then an illustration in computer memory can be "imported" into the desktop program. A printer (black-and-white or color) attached to the computer would produce the final pages.

Always **proofread** the final pages to check design of text and illustrations, spelling, and any omissions or incorrectly placed items. Have a person who has not been involved in the writing review them. He or she can catch errors you may have missed.

Reproduction

Once the master pages are completed, copies can be made. Most organizations use a photocopy machine for reproduction. You may have a choice of paper in various colors. At times this can be important for separating sections or calling attention to special pages.

Be sure to file the master pages for future use. If a desktop publishing program is used, save the master disk.

Collate, hole punch, and assemble pages for distribution to students. Materials can be stapled, bound, or put in notebooks for use.

Using Printed Materials

For instructional purposes, printed materials can be used at any time. You may distribute a notebook or study guide containing materials for reference and use at the start of a course. Have students turn to the necessary sheets when ready to use them. Or, during a class period, distribute the materials just before you will refer to them. This avoids the practice of students reading materials while you are discussing another topic. For out-of-class activities, decide when materials should best be made available to students.

Summary

1. Printed materials for training include handouts, worksheets, study guides, manuals, information sheets, and reprints of articles.

2. Permission to reproduce copyrighted materials should be obtained.

3. When preparing printed materials, refer to your stated objectives, knowledge or skill level to be developed, and the preparation level of students.

4. Consider choice of words that will communicate most effectively and illustrations to help understanding.

5. Assemble words and illustrations as the "master" pages.

6. Reproduce, organize, and distribute materials for convenient use.

Review Exercise

1. Which statements are TRUE about printed materials?
____ a. Handouts may be given to students at any time.
____ b. Consider saving your "master" so that additional copies can be prepared as needed in the future.
____ c. Pay careful attention to the use of headings as a way to help students identify separate sections of printed materials.
____ d. Keep paragraphs short and to the point.
____ e. Using colored paper for printed material is an unnecessary luxury.

2. Which is NOT a purpose for using illustrations in printed materials?
____ a. Make material attractive.
____ b. Substitute for a lengthy, verbal explanation.
____ c. Clarify information expressed in words.
____ d. Fill space or even out columns on a page.
____ e. Show how to carry-out a procedure.

3. Which of the following suggestions are included in this chapter?
____ a. Use colored lettering in preference to black lettering.
____ b. Use rubber cement to adhere an illustration to a page.
____ c. Be consistent in capitalization and abbreviations.
____ d. Use headings.
____ e. Use technical terms as frequently as possible since students will understand them by this repeated use.

Answers: 1. b,c,d.
      2. d.
      3. b,c,d.

References

Creating Effective Manuals. J. D'Agenais and J. Carruthers. Cincinnati, OH: South-Western Publishing, 1986.

Design Principles for Desktop Publishing. T. Lichty. Glenview, IL: Scott Foresman, 1989.

"Designing Electronic Text: The Role of Print-Based Research." J. Hartley. *Educational Communications and Technology Journal,* 1987, *35* (1), 3-17.

Designing Instructional Text. J. Hartley. New York: Nichols, 1987.

"Designing Manuals for Active Learning Styles." B. Mirel, S. Feinberg, and L. Allmendeiger. *Technical Communications,* 1991, *38* (First Quarter), 75-87.

Desktop Publishing by Design. R. Shushan. Redmond, WA: Microsoft Press, 1989.

"Making Instructional Materials Readable." E. T. Parker. *Performance and Instruction,* 1989, *28*(4), 26-27.

Preparing Instructional Text: Document Design Using Desktop Publishing. E. R. Misanchuk. Englewood Cliffs, NJ: Educational Technology Publications, 1992.

Text Display: Analysis and Systematic Design. G. L. Gropper. Englewood Cliffs, NJ: Educational Technology Publications, 1991.

Chapter 10

OVERHEAD TRANSPARENCIES

In this chapter you will learn to:

> • **Identify features that make the overhead projector a useful training device.**
> • **Design transparencies for class use.**
> • **Use four methods for preparing transparencies.**
> • **Recognize special techniques for use with transparencies.**
> • **Complete and file transparencies.**
> • **Plan an effective classroom presentation using the overhead projector.**

Overhead transparencies are inexpensive sheets of film measuring 8 1/2"x11" which contain images that are projected on a screen with an overhead projector. Depending on the film used, images may include written or printed material, line drawings, charts, or photographs in full color.

Features

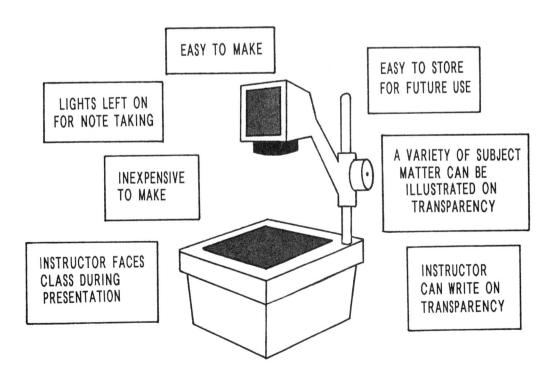

Planning Transparencies

In deciding to use transparencies in training, this media planning procedure should be followed:

- Verify the need for transparencies.
- State the objectives to be accomplished.
- Outline the content to be treated.

Then, keep the following in mind as you design each transparency:

- Limit transparency content to a single concept or part of a subject.
- Develop a series of related transparencies rather than crowd too much material on a single transparency.
- Try using no more than six words per line and no more than eight lines per transparency.
- Use lettering *at least* one-quarter inch tall on the original (often called the master). This can be prepared with a word processing computer program, lettering machine, or by hand lettering. Regular typewriting or print in books and magazines often are not directly readable on transparencies.

> # LETTERING AT LEAST THIS HIGH

- Except for short captions, use lower case words for ease of reading.
- Design transparencies in a horizontal format to insure that students will be able to see the lower part of the projected material. Low ceilings or light fixtures are sometimes in the way of a projected image that is oriented vertically.
- Enlarge diagrams and printed material from books and magazines to the proper size, using a photocopy machine before making the transparency.
- Consider using color on those parts of a transparency which need to be emphasized.

Preparing Transparencies

Many processes have been developed for making transparencies. They range from simple hand lettering on clear film to methods requiring special equipment and technical skills. It is important to select the transparency film specifically designed for the equipment to be used. The most practical techniques are described here.

On Clear Film   On paper, make a sketch or diagram, or prepare lettering which will be the content of your finished transparency. Place a sheet of clear film (also called **acetate**) over the paper and trace information onto the film using a fine-tipped felt pen. Some felt pens are waterbased, while others contain permanent ink. (See page 75.) Waterbased marks are easily erased with a wet cloth while permanent felt pen lines are difficult to remove. Read the label!

Felt pens also can be used to color words, parts, or areas of a black-line transparency. With a waterbased felt pen, marks can be made on any transparency during use. Erase the marks with a damp cloth.

With a Photocopy Machine   With the appropriate film for the brand of photocopier in your office, transparencies can be prepared from most printed or drawn illustrations. Colors, other than black on the original, will reproduce as gray. Place a single sheet of film in the paper feed tray and expose to the original.

Some copy machines, usually available at photocopy centers, can be used to prepare full-color transparencies.

With Thermal Film

With a thermal copy machine (3M or similar brand), transparencies can be made from original material having a carbon base. The use of a soft-lead pencil, newspaper, magazine, or book pages, and material prepared with a photocopy machine, will all work well as the lines contain the necessary carbon. Be alert to letter size limitations as explained previously.

If the original does *not* contain carbon-based lines, this can be remedied by making a duplicate copy on a photocopy machine. This copy will contain carbon lines which will reproduce in a thermal transparency maker.

In addition to black image film for thermal copy machines, various colored-image films are available. Follow instructions for the proper settings. Place the thermal film on top of the original and feed the two into the machine.

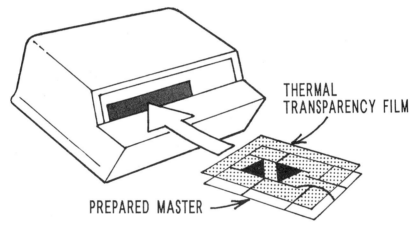

THERMAL TRANSPARENCY FILM

PREPARED MASTER →

With a Computer

Many types of visual materials can be created with a word processing, graphics, or desktop publishing program and a personal computer. Examples of such programs are *Aldus Freehand, Adobe Persuasion, Corel Draw,* and *MacDraw.* From the data stored on a disk, a paper copy or a transparency can be printed in high quality with a laser printer.

With other computer printers, make a paper copy. Intensify the image by reproducing with a photocopier. Then make the transparency on the copier or a thermal machine.

An alternative is to project the information directly from computer memory with an overhead projector. This requires the use of an electronic unit called a **computer projection panel** that consists of a **liquid crystal display** (LCD). The unit, which looks like a glass window the size of an overhead transparency, is plugged into the microcomputer monitor output and placed on the glass stage of the projector. When an image is called up from the data file on the disk, it appears on the window and is immediately projected onto the screen. By using the computer keyboard, the image can be modified while it is being viewed by the class. Make certain lettering is large enough for suitable legibility.

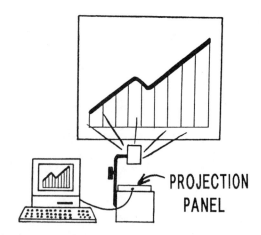

PROJECTION
PANEL

Special Instructional Techniques with Transparencies

In addition to placing a transparency on the projector and showing all of its content, you can use a number of techniques that would enhance effective communication. They require that you smoothly manipulate material on the glass plate of the projector. Become familiar with the following suggestions. Prepare materials and then practice before using them in the classroom.

Revelation Control the rate of projecting information by placing a sheet of paper *under* the transparency. Then set both on the projector's stage. During use, pull the under sheet down, thus exposing each line or area as you discuss it. This keeps the students' attention on what you are explaining, rather than showing all the information at the same time.

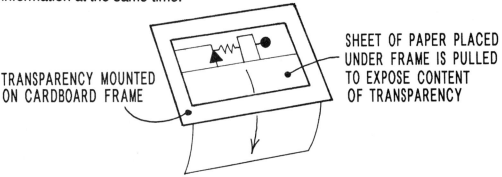

TRANSPARENCY MOUNTED
ON CARDBOARD FRAME

SHEET OF PAPER PLACED
UNDER FRAME IS PULLED
TO EXPOSE CONTENT
OF TRANSPARENCY

Another technique is to cover sections of a transparency with pieces of cardboard and tape each one to the transparency's cardboard frame. Turn back each mask when ready to present that part of the content.

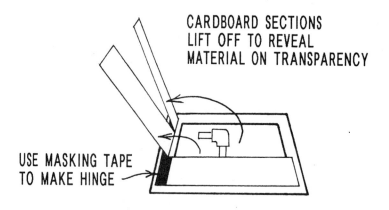

CARDBOARD SECTIONS
LIFT OFF TO REVEAL
MATERIAL ON TRANSPARENCY

USE MASKING TAPE
TO MAKE HINGE

Overlays After locating or preparing a detailed subject on paper, a decision can be made to divide the content into logical parts. Prepare each part on separate sheets of paper, each one carefully aligned over the original drawing. Copy each sheet on transparency film. Mount all sheets on a frame as explained below. Show them sequentially, one over the other, building to the complete subject.

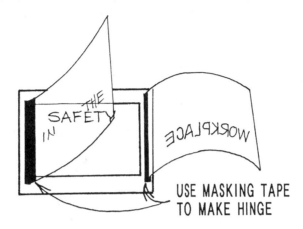

This can be a dramatic way to present information. Overlay transparencies capture and hold attention of students and allow you to clearly explain a subject having much detail.

Completing and Filing Transparencies

Once transparencies are completed, they can be used as is or mounted in a frame for ease of handling. If they are to remain unmounted, each film should be separated with a sheet of paper because of static charges that will make adjacent film sheets adhere together. Also, with paper underneath, individual transparencies can be visually identified before being placed on the projector.

Mounting By taping a transparency to the underside of a cardboard frame, it becomes more durable and easily handled. If overlays are to be shown, then mounting is essential. Align each overlay in proper position over the transparency base sheet that is taped to the underside of the frame. Fasten each overlay with tape along an edge on the upper side of the frame.

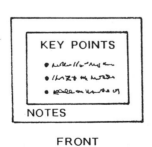 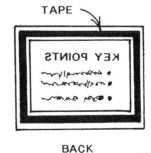

Write brief notes along the margin of the frame for reference during use.

Filing   Transparencies mounted in frames can be stored in a standard filing cabinet. Organize them under appropriate subject or topic headings. Unmounted transparencies can be placed in clear, plastic folders for protection and filed in a three-ring binder.

Using the Overhead Projector

When using the overhead projector, the instructor faces the class from the front of the room, maintaining eye contact, while projecting transparencies in a lighted room. Here are some suggestions for making a smooth, professional presentation:

• Place the projector on a chair or low stand so it will not block view of the screen by any member of the class. Set it far enough from the screen so the projected image completely fills the screen.
• Position the screen high enough so all members of the class can easily see your visuals. Bottom of projected image should be at student eye level and extend upward on the screen.
• Adjust blinds or window shades so that distracting light from windows does not strike the screen.
• Turn off lights at front of the room that may reflect directly off the screen and reduce image brilliance.
• Plan to stand or sit beside the projector as you show transparencies.
• Do not block the projected light from the lens with your body as you show transparencies.
• Arrange transparencies in proper order for use.
• Avoid hand movements over the transparency, causing annoying distractions on the screen.
• Remain at the projector, facing the class, and indicate items on the transparency with a pencil or a small pointer. Do this rather than walk to the screen and point to the projected image.
• As you show a transparency, use a waterbased colored felt pen to mark items or add lines and words.
• Turn off the projection lamp when not needed, such as between showing transparencies, or finished with projection.
• Blackout the screen by taping a square of cardboard to the top of the projection lens. Flip the cardboard down over the lens to interrupt the light path. Raise it to the topside of the lens when ready to show the next transparency. (Be sure to leave a transparency on the stage to absorb heat when the mask is over the lens.)

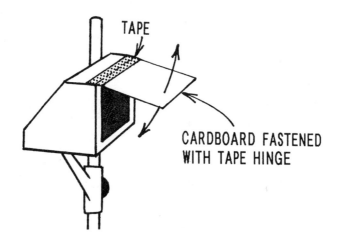

TAPE

CARDBOARD FASTENED
WITH TAPE HINGE

Using a Video Presentation Stand

A device that looks like an overhead projector is called a video presentation stand. It has a small video camera where the mirror and lens are located. Not only overhead transparencies, but slides, regular pictures, diagrams in a book, and even real objects can be shown on a television monitor or on a large screen if the unit is connected to a video projector (page 113).

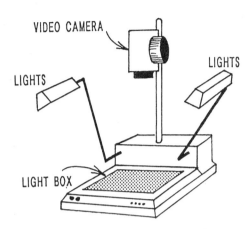

While a built-in illuminator is used with slides and transparencies, a pair of auxiliary lights provides illumination for opaque items. The zoom lens on the video camera provides flexibility for closeup details of materials placed under the camera.

Summary

1. The overhead projector supports the use of many simple techniques for making effective classroom presentations.

2. Transparencies should be carefully planned to take into consideration amount of material to be shown, suitable lettering styles and sizes, inclusion of illustrations, and using colors.

3. Transparency preparation methods include marking directly on clear film with felt pens, in a photocopy or thermal machine, or with a computer.

4. Techniques of revelation and use of overlays can be applied with transparencies.

5. Transparencies can be mounted in cardboard frames, or stored in plastic folders, and filed under appropriate headings.

6. The overhead projector is used in a lighted room as the instructor faces the class from front of the room.

Review Exercise

1. Which statements are TRUE about planning overhead transparencies?
___ a. Preferably design transparencies in vertical format.
___ b. Use lower case lettering for other than short captions.
___ c. Use at least one-quarter inch high lettering.
___ d. Color is unnecessary on most transparencies.
___ e. For a complex topic, develop a series of transparencies.
___ f . A small illustration can be enlarged on many office copy machines.
___ g. Overlays should be used with simple subject transparencies.

2. To which transparency-preparation process does each relate?
___ a. Directly with felt pens.
___ b. With a machine most often available in an office.
___ c. Original must be prepared with a soft lead pencil.
___ d. Use a word-processing program.
___ e. Use felt pens for adding color. (More than one answer possible.)
___ f . Can be immediately shown, once created, with a liquid display unit.
___ g. Uses film that easily reproduces a diagram in single colors in addition to black.

3. Which practices would you apply when using transparencies in a classroom?
___ a. Place the screen low so trainees need not strain to view images.
___ b. Set the projector on a low stand.
___ c. Stand beside the projector so you do not block the projection light to the screen.
___ d. Go to the screen to indicate parts of a transparency as you discuss it.
___ e. Before use, always tape transparencies in cardboard frames.
___ f . If possible, turn off lights at front of the room.
___ g. Uncover parts of a transparency by masking with an opaque material.
___ h. Control light output from the projector by covering the lens with a cardboard mask.

Answers: 1. b,c,e,f.
        2. a – clear film; b – photocopy machine; c – heat process; d – computer;
            e – all methods; f – computer; g – heat process.
        3. b,c,f,g,h.

References

Five Hundred Ways to Use the Overhead Projector. L. Green and D. Dengerink. Littleton, CO: Libraries Unlimited, 1982.

"CD Panels." *Electronic Learning*, 1991, *10*(6), 46-49.

Overhead Projection. J.D. Sparks. Englewood Cliffs, NJ: Educational Technology Publications, 1981.

Planning, Producing, and Using Instructional Technologies. J.E. Kemp and D.C. Smellie. New York: HarperCollins, 1993.

Chapter 11

SLIDES and SLIDE/TAPE PROGRAMS

In this chapter you will learn to:

> • **Identify features that make slides useful in training.**
> • **Plan slides and a slide/tape program.**
> • **Prepare slides and a slide/tape program.**
> • **Utilize slides and a slide/tape program in training.**

The 35mm slide, commonly called the **"2x2,"** is an excellent way to present subject matter in a colorful and realistic manner. As with all projected media, the slide centers student attention on the important points you wish to emphasize. Slides are relatively inexpensive and easy to make.

Features

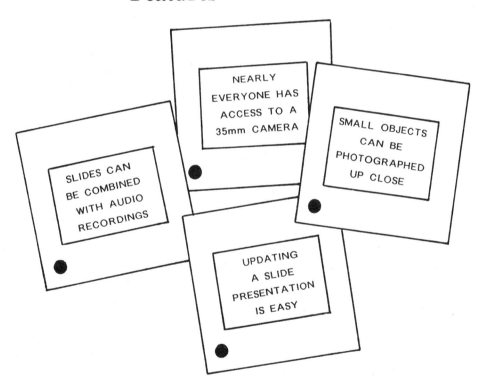

Planning an Instructional Slide Program

While an instructor can prepare a number of individual slides to illustrate specific points, a set of carefully planned, sequentially arranged slides on a topic, can be an effective instructional resource. To accomplish this, the following planning procedure is suggested.

Preliminary Planning

- Determine whether or not slides are appropriate for the topic. See page 54 for questions that help you make the decision.
- List the objectives. They will identify what the students should know or be able to do after seeing the slides. See Chapter 3.
- Analyze the audience. What basic knowledge and skills do students have? What do they already know about the topic? See Chapter 4.
- Organize the content of the slides by reviewing the objectives. List items to be covered. This becomes the content outline (page 12). Remember that the content helps to accomplish the objectives.

Storyboard

Decide what visuals are needed to tell the "story" as presented in the content outline. A storyboard can help to visualize and arrange the content for effective communication. It consists of a series of sketches that represents the pictures, along with narration notes. See example on page 107.

The storyboard identifies the "shots" that need to be made to insure that the audience will understand what is to be presented. To do this, the following types of shots would be considered:

- **Establishing Shot** (ES) or **Long Shot** (LS)
  A general overview of the setting and the subject.
- **Medium Shot** (MS)
  A closer look at the main subject, eliminating unnecessary background and other details.
- **Closeup Shot** (CU)
  A close-in look at the main subject, concentrating on details.

Script

Script preparation comes next. It includes the actual narration for each scene. Although plans may include your talking as the slides are being shown, a script will help to guide the presentation. See example of script on page 107 and suggestions under Planning a Recording on page 99.

It is extremely important to determine which will carry the message ... the audio or the visual. They should never be equal in impact. The role can change many times during a slide presentation.

Producing Slides and Slide/Tape Program

The preparation of a slide presentation or a slide/tape program involves a number of activities:

- Select film for slides.
- Prepare graphics, including titles and illustrations.
- Photograph titles and scenes as shown in the storyboard.
- Process film into slides.
- Select the best slides and place them in a carousel tray.
- Check scripted narration against final slides for any necessary word changes.
- Record narration on audiotape.
- Add synchronizing signals on tape to cue slide changes when an appropriate tape recorder is connected to a slide projector.

**Preparing
to Film**

- Select film for the light conditions under which you will take pictures. A faster film (higher index or ISO number) would be required under low light conditions. For help, visit a photo supply store, or review the camera's instructional booklet.
- Understand the proper use of your camera. Consult your owner's manual.
- Recognize that a single-lens reflex (SLR) camera is preferred to a camera with a window viewfinder for making closeup shots.
- Use a SLR camera on a copystand or attached to a tripod for filming titles, artwork, graphs, and illustrations. When photographing small subjects, a closeup lens may be needed.
- Closeup copywork may result in incorrectly exposed film. Avoid this by placing a neutral gray test card (obtained from a photo supply store) on the material under the camera. Allow the light meter on the camera to read the light reflected from the gray card. Use this exposure to determine the camera setting for all copywork under these lighting conditions.
- When preparing titles, leave plenty of area around the lettering. This is referred to as "bleed space." It will ensure that the camera will photograph the lettering without seeing the cardboard or paper edge.

**Shoot
Pictures**

- Select a shutter speed (at least 1/60th second) to avoid blurred pictures due to camera movement. For slower shutter speeds, attach the camera to a tripod.
- Take more than a single shot for any scene in which you feel the composition, action, or exposure should be varied. Select the best "take" when you view the slides.
- Try to shoot all pictures with the camera held in a horizontal position so all slides will project the same format on the screen. This is especially important if slides will be copied to videotape for use as described on page 97.
- An **electronic still camera** (also called a **still video camera**) can record slide images on a two-inch disk. The resulting slides are viewed on a computer screen or on a television receiver via a photo CD player. With the necessary equipment, these slide images can be copied, rearranged, enhanced, and even enlarged. Also, they can be used in a computer graphics program.

**Record
Narration**

After viewing the final slides, make any necessary word changes in the script. Note recommendations on page 99 for preparing the narration so it will clearly communicate the information you wish to present. A carefully written audio script can enhance a slide presentation.

Refer to the suggestions for recording procedure in Chapter 12. The method for adding signals on tape to synchronize slide changes with the narration is also described.

Using Slides and Slide/Tape Program

When slides are ready to be loaded into the carousel tray, each one should be coded with a "thumbspot" in the lower left corner as the slide is viewed correctly. After the thumbspot has been made with a pen or felt marker, rotate the slide until it is upside down. The thumbspot will now be in the upper right hand corner.

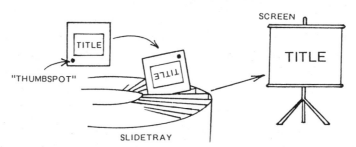

While facing the screen, place all slides into the tray in this upside-down position as shown. This technique will ensure that slides will be loaded correctly, thus avoiding images that appear improperly on the screen (upside-down or backwards). As soon as all slides are loaded into the tray, lock the retaining ring in position on top of the tray.

- Fill the screen with the projected image by adjusting the zoom lens on the projector, or move the projector until the image fills the screen.
- Make certain the bottom of the projected image is no lower than the head level of the audience.
- A small pen light would be helpful in locating projector/tape recorder controls in a darkened room.
- Locate the room light switch and prearrange for someone to lower the lights on cue.
- Check all cable connections. Make certain that the audio is functioning and that the slides advance on cue.
- If you are planning to control slide changes from the front of the room, use an extension on the remote control cable.
- Do not start or end a presentation with a bright light on the screen. This is distracting to the audience. If the projector is not the type that automatically goes to black when there is no slide in projection position, use blank 2x2 pieces of cardboard to block out the light. Place one at the beginning of the slide series and one at the end.
- With the use of a **programmer** and a **dissolve unit**, two slide projectors can be operated so that the light in one projector fades out while the other one fades in. The image from one slide appears as the previous one disappears. This "dissolve" technique creates a smooth visual flow as compared with a sudden black screen between adjacent slides when a single projector is used.
- Students will not be able to take notes in a darkened room, so you may want to pause the presentation and turn on lights every so often to allow for note-taking and to discuss key points.
- A handout could serve as a summary for the slide program.
- Consider the possibility of using a slide program in conjunction with other forms of media, such as overhead transparencies or even the chalkboard. The slide program can be stopped at any time for you to refer to other material. Return to the slides when ready.
- Make a duplicate set of slides and audio recording. This will serve as protection in case of loss or damage.

Transferring Slide Program to Videotape

An instructor may find it more convenient to use a video recording of a slide program rather than the slides themselves. This transfer can be done commercially at a nominal fee. The procedure directly transmits the slide image to videotape. But if funds are not available, it is easy to project the slides onto a screen and copy to videotape yourself. Record the sound at the same time.

Follow this procedure:

- Adjust the slide projector so that approximately a two-foot picture is projected.

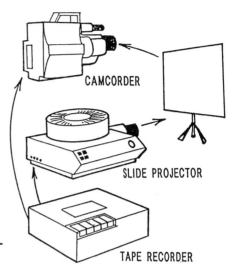

CAMCORDER

SLIDE PROJECTOR

TAPE RECORDER

- Use a camcorder or set up a video camera and recorder. Place the camera directly over the slide projector, aimed at the screen. Fill the viewfinder with the image of the slide picture on the screen and focus.
- Attach connecting cables from the audiotape player (output) to the video recorder (input) for recording sound.
- Run ten seconds of videotape as "leader" before the slide program starts.
- After recording, play the program to check that pictures and sound are on the tape correctly.

The transfer and use of a videotape recording eliminates the possibility that any slides might be lost, projected incorrectly, or, most important, having pictures and narration out of synchronization when the slide program is shown.

Summary

1. An advantage of using slides for training is that they represent an inexpensive way to put large, colorful pictures on a screen for the entire class to see at the same time.

2. Plan a slide program by defining objectives, developing a content outline, planning shots as a storyboard, and writing a script that includes a description of each scene along with the narration.

3. Prepare the slide program by carefully: selecting film, preparing titles and illustrations, shooting the pictures including copystand work, recording narration, adding sync signals, and making a duplicate of the program.

4. Prepare to use the slide program by "thumbspotting" slides, setting up equipment, planning handouts, arranging for class discussion, and considering coordinated use of other media.

5. Consider transferring the slide program to videotape for ease of use in the classroom.

Review Exercise

1. In what order should these planning steps for a slide program take place?
____ a. Organize subject content.
____ b. Analyze preparation of students in the class.
____ c. Write the script.
____ d. Decide that slides are suitable for the topic.
____ e. Develop a storyboard.
____ f. Write learning objectives.

2. In what order would you carry-out the following for preparing a slide/tape program. (Note: If you believe one or more steps are left out, add each one in the proper position.)

_____ a. Photograph titles and artwork.
_____ b. Choose film for use.
_____ c. Duplicate slides and tape, or copy program onto videotape.
_____ d. Check final program.
_____ e. Process film.
_____ f . Add sync signal to tape for slide changes.
_____ g. Prepare titles and artwork.
_____ h. Place slides in slide tray.
_____ i . Select best slide for each scripted scene.

3. Which practices are appropriate when a slide program is used?

_____ a. Arrange to turn off room lights before starting.
_____ b. Start and end the program with bright light on the screen to get attention.
_____ c. If you show slides yourself, have a long remote control cable to front of the room.
_____ d. Project a large picture on the screen.
_____ e. Have students make notes after the program is ended.
_____ f . Check the sync between slides and narration before you start.

4. What procedure can be used to duplicate a slide/tape program for use and be certain it is both easy to use and will not lose synchronization between slides and the sound?

Answers: 1. d,b,f,a,e,c.
         2. (1) – b; (2) – take pictures according to storyboard or script; (3) – g; (4) – a; (5) – e; (6) – i; (7) – h; (8) – revise narration as necessary; (9) – record narration; (10) – f; (11) – d; (12) – c.
         3. a,c,d,f.
         4. Copy slides and recording onto videotape.

References

Creating Slide Presentations. J.R. Podracky. Englewood Cliffs, NJ: Prentice-Hall, 1983.

Creative Slide/Tape Programs. L. Green. Englewood, CO: Libraries Unlimited, 1986.

Effective Lecture Slides. Publication S-22. Rochester, NY: Eastman Kodak Co., 1988.

Planning, Producing, and Using Learning Technologies. J.E. Kemp and D.C. Smellie. New York: HarperCollins, 1993.

"Slide to Tape Transfer." J. B. Brandt. *Media and Methods,* 1991, *27*(9), 16, 38.

Slides: Planning and Producing Slide Programs. Rochester, NY: Eastman Kodak Co., 1989.

"Viewing Slides on Your VCR." M. Hershenson. *Industrial Photography,* 1991, *40*(2), 20, 54.

Chapter **12**

AUDIOTAPE RECORDINGS

In this chapter you will learn to:

- Plan an instructional audiotape recording.
- Select and use a microphone.
- Make an audiotape recording.
- Protect the recording against accidental erasure.
- Add a signal to the tape for changing slides during a presentation.
- Use audio recordings in the classroom.

There are many potential uses for audio materials in training. An important speech, an interview with an expert, a description of a demonstration, or the explanation of a procedure are some purposes for which you might bring a recording into class for analysis and discussion. Such recordings also can allow students to study or review content on their own.

Features

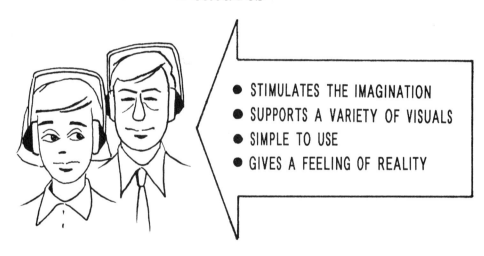

- STIMULATES THE IMAGINATION
- SUPPORTS A VARIETY OF VISUALS
- SIMPLE TO USE
- GIVES A FEELING OF REALITY

Planning a Recording

In preparation for a recording, follow the usual media planning procedure described on page 70. Then check the script carefully, choosing the best word or phrase for quick understanding. Remember that hearing narration is not like being able to reread the printed page.

Here are suggestions when writing the script:

- Be conversational by writing the narration in simple, easy-to-understand phrases, and straightforward English ... the way people talk.

99

- Avoid expressions like "here we see," or "in the next slide..." There is no need to tell the viewer what will be seen when it is obvious.
- Keep sentences short (10–15 words) and avoid multiple clauses.
- In a sentence, place the subject and verb close together for ease in understanding.
- Avoid tongue-twisting expressions or awkward-sounding phrases.
- Have some pauses in narration, otherwise the student will stop listening in a short time.
- Realize that one bit of narration can cover a number of pictures, and that narration can carry over from one scene to the next.
- Finally, when the script is ready, read the narration aloud to test expressions, the pacing, and the emphasis on important words.

Making the Recording

Select a quiet location in which to make the recording. This means that traffic noise, outside voices, air conditioner hum, and other extraneous sounds are avoided. This will ensure a better quality recording.

Most light-weight tape recorders contain a built-in microphone that acts as a "sound-seeking" microphone. This means that during a time no one is talking, the tape recorder volume will automatically increase in order to record whatever sound is available. This can introduce unwanted sounds in your recording.

A better quality recording will result from attaching a separate microphone to the microphone input on the recorder and setting the volume manually for the anticipated sounds.

As preparation is made to start recording, consider these suggestions:

- Disconnect any telephone in the room so that it will not ring during the recording period.
- Place a sign on the outside of the door indicating that a recording session is in progress.
- Handle the microphone as little as possible. This will help to avoid unwanted noise. Attaching the microphone to a stand is always a good idea.
- Remove staples and paper clips from the script pages before starting to record. They cause paper rustling sounds that are easily picked up by the microphone. As one page is finished, quietly move to the next page by slipping the top page out of the way.
- If several people are involved in making the recording, communicate by using hand signals.

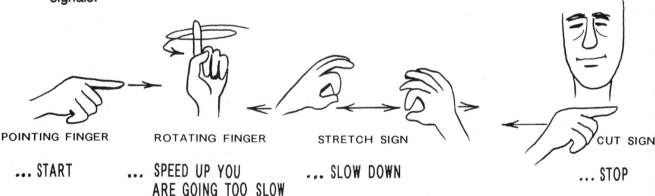

POINTING FINGER   ROTATING FINGER   STRETCH SIGN   CUT SIGN

... START   ... SPEED UP YOU ARE GOING TOO SLOW   ... SLOW DOWN   ... STOP

- Voices used in the recording should sound conversational and informal, not like the script is being read.
- Do not tilt your head down to read the script. Instead, hold the pages up so that the head

position is directed toward the microphone.

- When getting ready to record, move the tape forward in the cassette until the start of the brown recording tape can be seen ... not just the plastic leader. This will ensure that the recording will start on the tape.
- After the recording is completed, rewind and listen to it carefully. Check for any errors like variations from the script, improper speaking, and extraneous noise. Make any necessary corrections.
- Before starting, or immediately after completing the recording, identify the recording by writing a title or name on the cassette.
- Protect the recording against accidental erasure by snapping off the two tabs located on back of the cassette edge. If the tape is to be pulsed for use with slides, do *not* remove the tabs until *after* the sync signals have been put on the tape.

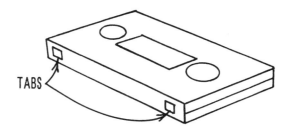

- It is always advisable to make a copy of the original recording to be used in class or by individual students. The original (the **master** recording) should be safely stored for additional copies in the future.

Slide Change Signals

If the recording is to be used in synchronization with a slide presentation, a signal should be added to the recording at those locations where slide changes are to be made. This can be done in two ways:

1. As the recording is being made, an **audible** signal can be added to the tape. The signal can be made with a buzzer, a bell, or some other device that makes a short, sharp sound. As the slides are shown along with the recording, the sound is heard and the person operating the projector advances to the next slide. Remember to allow at least one second for a slide change to take place.

2. The second method for recording a signal is preferred to the above method as it places an **inaudible** signal on the tape. Use a tape recorder equipped with a **pulse button** feature for adding the signal to the tape. *After* the voice recording has been completed, play the recording and press the pulse button each time a slide change is to be made. An inaudible signal is recorded on the second track of the tape. During use, the slide projector is connected to the same tape recorder. Then as the tape plays, slides are changed automatically. (No one will be able to hear this signal.)

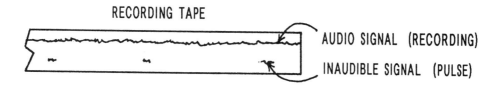

Using the Recording

Here are important suggestions when using an audio recording in training:

- Almost all portable audiocassette players have small speakers which limits the sound quality on playback. The quality of your presentation can be enhanced by using a larger speaker. Any loudspeaker from a film projector or sound system can be used. Attach the proper connecting cord from the tape recorder output to the speaker.
- Before starting to play the recording, preset the volume sound level and cue the tape to start without a long waiting period.
- Prepare the class for the listening activity. Tell students what they are going to hear and list the key points on the chalkboard or flipchart. A handout can be distributed containing a summary of the information presented.
- As appropriate, stop the tape at predetermined points for discussion and questions.
- Try playing the recording a second time for the class. Some details or subtle features could be missed or misunderstood the first time.
- Once the recording playback is concluded, allow time for class discussion and questions relating to the material presented.
- Audio recordings can also be used by students outside of class. Refer to suggestions for self-paced learning on page 119.

Summary

1. Determine that a recording is needed for training purposes.

2. List the objectives, outline the content, and prepare the script.

3. Make the recording, using a separate microphone, in a quiet area.

4. If the tape is to be used as part of a slide program, pulse the tape for automatic changes, or record an audible signal at the time the voice recording is made.

5. Duplicate the original recording for use, storing the master to make future copies.

6. During use in the classroom, prepare the group by outlining what they will hear. Display the key points. Consider a handout as a summary sheet.

7. Check equipment prior to playing the tape in the classroom. Use a larger, separate speaker for better sound quality.

8. Review what was heard, discuss, and answer questions.

9. Consider the use of audio recordings for study by individual students.

Review Exercise

1. In preparing a script for an audiotape recording, which practices are preferred?
____ a. Type the script double-spaced.
____ b. Move along as quickly as possible with the narration since the recording is made to save time.
____ c. Read the script aloud to check it before making the recording.
____ d. Speak into the microphone with an authoritative tone of voice.
____ e. Keep sentences short and avoid complex phrases.

2. In the following list, some procedures have been omitted that should be followed when making a recording. Add them between the appropriate steps.
a. Use a separate, good-quality microphone.
b. Disconnect a telephone that may be in the recording room.
c. Attach the microphone to a stand.
d. Use hand signals to communicate with persons reading the script during recording.
e. Hold the script up so sound from voice goes directly toward the microphone.

3. You have completed recording the narration. Now answer these questions:
a. What is the difference between *audible* and *inaudible* signals for slide changes?

b. Once the final recording is completed, what precaution should be taken to be certain the recording cannot be erased?

c. How would you use the recording with a class?

Answers: 1. a,c,e.
2. After **b** place "recording in progress" sign on door.
After **c** separate script pages to avoid rustling sound.
After **d** advance tape past the leader before recording.
3. a. Audible signal is created mechanically and heard, while inaudible signal is created electronically and automatically causes slide changes.
b. Punch out the tabs on back edge of the cassette.
c. Set up equipment, check playback of recording, introduce recording to class, summarize key points, discuss, and answer questions.

References

Audio in Media. S. R. Alten. Belmont, CA: Wadsworth, 1990.

Basic Audio Production: Theory, Equipment, and Techniques. M. Nelson. White Plains, NY: Knowledge Industry Publications, 1992.

"Design of the Audio Track for Instructional Slide Sets." D. Pett. *Performance and Instruction,* 1989, *28*(9), 1-4.

Planning, Producing, and Using Instructional Technologies. J. E. Kemp and D. C. Smellie. New York: HarperCollins, 1993.

Chapter **13**

VIDEO RECORDINGS

In this chapter you will learn how to:

> - **Recognize features which make video recording a widely used instructional resource for training.**
> - **Use basic video terms.**
> - **Plan a video recording, including storyboarding and scripting.**
> - **Make a video recording, including lighting scenes, shooting scenes with continuity, preparing graphics, and editing tape.**
> - **Take proper care of a camcorder.**
> - **Use video recordings in training.**

While television has been a part of our daily lives for some time, recent developments in the technology have caused dramatic changes. These changes are mainly in the size reduction of video cameras, in the lower cost and simplification of video equipment, and improvement in the quality of the video image. The **camcorder**, combining camera and recorder in a single unit, is now widely used for training purposes.

Features

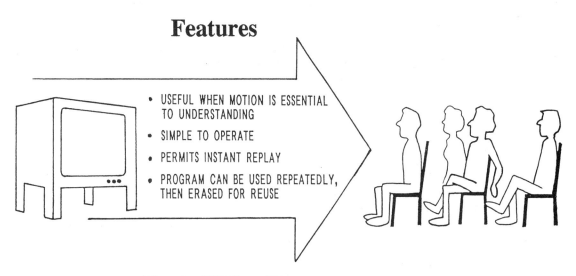

- USEFUL WHEN MOTION IS ESSENTIAL TO UNDERSTANDING
- SIMPLE TO OPERATE
- PERMITS INSTANT REPLAY
- PROGRAM CAN BE USED REPEATEDLY, THEN ERASED FOR REUSE

Basic Video Terms

Prior to any planning, it is important to understand the basic terms associated with the production of instructional video recordings. While not an exhaustive list, the terms described here are those which will be referred to in the following pages.

Shot or Scene   The basic element of video production, as measured each time the start button is activated and then released. It may cover an extended period of time, or be as short as a few seconds.

Sequence   A number of related shots or scenes put together to show a single event.

Establishing Shot (ES)   A view that establishes the location. It sets the time and place for the action to follow.

Long Shot (LS)   Similar to the ES, but more selective as it centers on the key elements of subject.

Medium Shot (MS)   A closer view of the subject or action. This shot isolates important elements of the subject, eliminating the less important.

   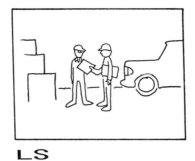   

ES   LS   MS

Closeup Shot (CU)   A more selective close view of specific details.

Extreme Closeup (ECU)   A very "tight" shot of a detail within the subject.

   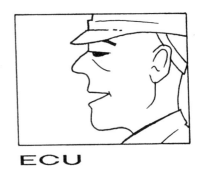

CU   ECU

High Angle Shot   The camera is raised over the subject, thus looking down on the action.

Low Angle Shot   The camera is placed low, thus looking up at the action.

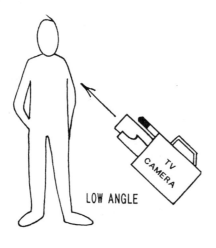   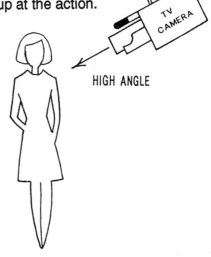

LOW ANGLE   HIGH ANGLE

Pan Shot	Camera movement either to the left or right, usually at a slow, steady pace.
Tilt Shot	Camera movement either up or down, usually at a slow, steady pace.
Zoom Shot	The use of a special lens (standard on many video cameras) which allows the camera to appear to move in on the action from a longer shot to a close-up or pull back from a closeup.

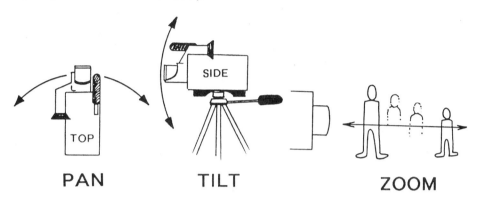

PAN   TILT   ZOOM

Storyboard	Cards on which visuals, in the form of sketches, are drawn as a guide to production. Notes regarding audio may be included.
Script	Specific directions for shooting scenes in the form of pages containing a list of scenes on the left with accompanying narration, or other audio effects, on the right.

STORYBOARD

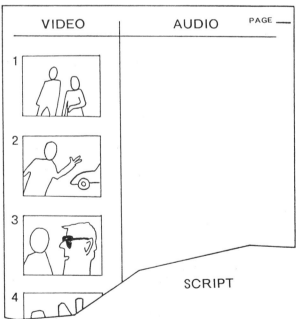

SCRIPT

To become familiar with the application of these terms, carefully watch the visual component of television programs. Turn off the sound and analyze how a variety of shots is used to communicate ideas and present information.

Video Training Styles

In terms of the objectives to be served, a video recording can be produced in one or a combination of these styles:

- **Interview** – Using a list of prepared questions, an interviewer asks an expert about the subject. Both information and personal experiences, relating to the subject, can be explored as the two persons are shown in conversation.

- **Demonstration** – A qualified person shows equipment and performs a skill. This individual can explain a procedure as the operation takes place, or an "off-camera" voice (a narrator), using a prepared script, describes what is being shown. Still pictures and slides may be part of the production.

- **Documentary** – By recording activities and situations as they normally take place, events and procedures can be shown realistically. A narrator's voice can interpret events as they are shown.

- **Dramatization** – An example of a scripted situation, like a simulation, using persons as actors, can be recorded for instructional or testing purposes.

Planning for Video Production

The planning phase should be completed before actual shooting begins. Assuming that the specific need for a video recording has been clearly established, plan for the following:

Title
If one has been chosen, write it down. If not, use the subject to be covered for identification and supply the actual title later.

Audience
Who will receive the "message" of the video recording? Careful audience identification and analysis are important. Review Chapter 4.

- Are there special needs of the audience?
- Are they bilingual?
- How much do they already know about the subject?

These and other questions about the audience should be considered as the plan for the video project proceeds.

Objectives
State clearly what the viewers will learn or be able to do after viewing the video recording. Review Chapter 3.

Content
After carefully reviewing the objectives, develop the content outline. This will be a listing of the content to be treated. Review Chapter 2.

Follow the above planning with the preparation of a **storyboard** and then writing a **script**.

Making the Video Recording

Nothing is apt to be more discouraging than viewing the results of the first attempt to shoot videotape. The picture zooms in and out, the image tilts occasionally, and the pan movements are jerky and uneven. What went wrong?

The following information will help to overcome many of the problems that plague the first attempts at videotaping. There are some basic rules and procedures which, if carefully followed, will produce acceptable results.

First, examine the instructional manual that comes with the camcorder. It should take but a short time to learn where the controls are located. Once you have mastered them, you can concentrate on the actual shooting.

Concept of Motion

Making a video recording is similar to preparing other instructional media. But a major difference becomes apparent when you start recording. The difference lies in the word MOTION. Movement can be accomplished by action within a scene, by change of camera angles and distances to the subject, by camera movement, by varying the length of scenes, or by combinations of these elements.

Camera Pan or Tilt

It will not always be possible to use a tripod, but do so whenever you can, especially for pan and tilt movements. This will make for smooth results. If the camcorder must be hand held, practice standing in such a way that you have good balance while still rotating your body. Try setting your feet in the direction toward which you will be panning before activating the camera. Press the start button and *slowly* pan in the direction you have chosen, ending with the camcorder facing the same direction as your feet.

Camera Zoom

The zoom should be used sparingly, although one or more zoom actions may be vital parts of the production. Often a better way to shoot would be to stop the camcorder between each shot, set the next scene in the viewer, and then continue to record.

Maintaining Continuity

Follow the sequence of scenes described in your storyboard. When one shot leads logically and easily to the next one, you have smooth **continuity** in the details of your story. Matching the action and maintaining the same screen direction between adjacent scenes contribute to continuity. Also, continuity is accomplished by smooth **transitions** from one sequence to the next by using titles or special visual effects like a fade-out/in or a dissolve (overlapping fade-out/fade-in) between scenes or sequences. See the camera's instruction manual.

By varying the shots (long, medium, closeup) you can maintain viewer interest. Be sure to place the camera so the viewer can easily see what is important in the scene. Variations like shooting over the shoulder of a person in the scene, rather than directly toward the subject, can be useful.

109

Shot Length No one can tell you how long a scene should be. In many instances the amount of time for the necessary action to take place sets the length. Other shots can be as short as two seconds. A static subject (non-action) viewed for longer than five seconds can reduce viewer attention. Sometimes the length of the narration indicates the scene time for a shot.

When everything is set and you are ready to shoot, remember to keep both eyes open when looking through the camera viewfinder. This is preferable to closing one eye and squinting into the viewfinder.

Lighting Video Scenes

Watching a video recording is actually seeing a two-dimensional picture which appears as a three-dimensional image because of the lighting in the original scene. For outdoor, daylight scenes, natural lighting from the sun creates the three-dimensional effect. For outdoor, night scenes or indoor shots, special lighting is needed. By using lights properly, the three-dimensional quality needed to portray reality can be created.

While you might use artificial lights just to raise the general illumination in a room, the properly lighted scenes utilize three basic lights.

Key Light This is the **main** source of light for a scene. The **key** light is placed to the side of the video camera, above eye level, and aimed at the subject.

Fill Light This light softens or eliminates shadows produced by the key light. The **fill** light is positioned on the other side of the camera from the key light and at the height of the camera. It is one-half the intensity of the key light.

Back Light This light separates the person or object from the background and may accent the facial features and hair of a subject. The **back** light is placed behind and above the subject. It is one-half the intensity of the key light.

The special lights used for television production have limited life. When not actually shooting, turn them off. Do not move lights while they are hot. Make every effort to handle lighting equipment with care to avoid lamp breakage.

Preparing Graphics for Video Production

The selection of good graphic materials, including titles, can do much to enhance a program. Poor graphics, on the other hand, can spoil an otherwise excellent recording.

In selecting or preparing any kind of graphic, it is important to remember that the visual must fit the format of the standard television viewing area. The format utilizes a ratio of **3 units HIGH** to **4 units WIDE**.

Sources of Readymade Materials

Many usable materials already exist in the form of charts, maps, and flipcharts. Usually these do not conform to the proper format. They can be effectively used if each one is placed on a bulletin board or on an easel where the person appearing in the scene can refer to it.

Slides and overhead transparencies, containing lettering, illustrations, or photographs, make excellent visuals for television. They can be projected on a screen so that the camera will pick up the image.

Commercially-prepared, copyright-free art called "clip art" can be used directly or adapted for inclusion in visuals for a video production. Clip art booklets on many subjects are found in art supply stores and as collections in computer graphics software programs.

Preparing Original Materials

Original drawings, cartoons, and lettering can be prepared for television. In selecting lettering styles, either Gothic or Roman styles can be used. Avoid script, Old English, or other hard to read styles.

Lettering should be large enough to be seen easily on the video screen. This means that words in a line of lettering should occupy at least 1/25th the height of the video monitor area. Space between lines of lettering should be approximately the same as the height of the lettering. Do not try to put more than six lines of lettering in a visual.

Keep the important parts of a visual (picture and lettering) away from the edges of the video area because receivers distort varying amounts at the edges.

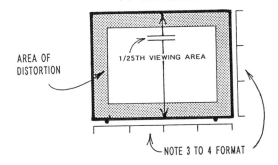

Editing the Recording

The newer video recorders have reached a level of technical excellence which permits you to move from one shot to the next shot without an annoying **glitch** (interference with the image like a break-up or rolling of the picture) appearing between the two scenes. This is a distinct advantage for it may enable you to complete the program in the camera without any follow-up editing.

Occasionally, however, it may be necessary to rearrange or shorten shots, delete certain sections, or add titles. The editing procedure is also necessary when you want to combine shots from more than a single tape into the final video recording. In editing, you electronically copy selected scenes, in proper order, from the original onto a second tape. Special equipment is available to carry-out the editing procedure. If detailed editing of your tapes becomes necessary, obtain assistance or instruction from someone with experience.

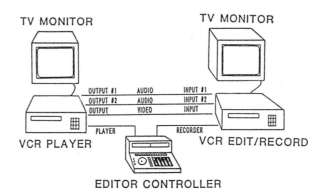

Always make a duplicate copy of a video recording that will be used in training. Two interconnected VCRs, as used in editing, are operated for the duplication. Store the original recording for future copies.

Camcorder Care

Taking care of the camcorder involves common sense. Avoid bumping or jarring the unit. If treated with respect and by performing simple maintenance, the equipment should continue to produce good results for a long time.

Moisture   Protect the camcorder from dampness with a plastic cover when it is not in use.

When moving equipment between locations having an extreme temperature difference, wait for the unit to adjust before using it. If not, condensation can form on the lens and other parts become damp.

Dirt and Dust If the camcorder has been exposed to dirt or dust, be sure to clean exposed parts and check operation.

Batteries   Camcorders use a nickel-cadmium battery which is rechargeable. Keep a standby battery fully charged. When not in use, remove the battery from the camcorder and store it in a cool place.

**Camcorder
Lens**

Camcorder lenses, like all camera lenses, are carefully ground pieces of glass with a protective coating (appearing as a purple tint) to cut out glare. Clean lenses only with lens cleaning tissue. Nothing else!

An ultraviolet (UV) filter or a skylight filter placed over the lens is an excellent way to protect it and to eliminate the problems of haze in long shot exterior scenes. Keep lens capped when not in use.

Heat

Camcorders should not be stored where there is excess heat, as in the trunk of a vehicle, on the dashboard of a car, or in direct sunlight, for an extended period of time. Excessive heat can seriously damage plastic parts of the camcorder body and internal mechanism. The same warnings apply to storing videocassettes. A padded carrying case makes an excellent protective container for shipping or moving the equipment.

Magnetism

The camcorder is a device that uses magnetism in the recording process. Therefore, it is important to keep it and recorded videotape away from electrical devices. Transformers, radio transmitters, generators, and high voltage equipment can cause problems.

Using Video Recordings

While this chapter refers to the production of video recordings to serve your training objectives, an instructor should be aware that there may be local sources of prepared recordings. This may be in your organization or available from a regional or statewide collection. Check catalogs for recordings relating to topics in your course. (See list on page 69.)

If you will be using a video recording you have not seen for sometime, or one with which you are unfamiliar, preview it to be certain it fits your learning objectives. Handout materials to accompany the video should be ready for use.

Occasionally a large picture is needed because of the number of viewers. Project a large image onto a regular screen by using a video projector attached to a videocassette player.

Instead of allowing students to sit passively, watching the complete recording, you may find it advantageous to stop the tape at the end of each segment to:

* ask questions and discuss with the class what was shown;
* allow time for students to write responses to worksheet questions;
* summarize the segment and introduce the next segment before viewing continues;
* invite student comments.

Also, allow individual students to review the recording on their own, after class. A second viewing can strengthen understanding and correct any misconceptions acquired the first time.

Other things to consider:

* From time to time before use, clean the heads of the video player, according to the owner's manual, so the best possible image will be seen.
* As with all visuals planned for class use, make certain that all students can clearly see the monitor and hear the sound.

- Keep reflection off the surface of the TV monitor by slightly turning the monitor to avoid direct light.
- Remember that other forms of media and activities, such as transparencies, slides, handouts, and class discussion, can be combined with a video presentation.
- Store the videocassette in a vertical position. This keeps pressure on the edges of the tape to a minimum, preventing stretching and curling that can distort picture and sound.

Summary

1. Video is most useful for training when subject motion needs visual treatment.

2. Several video terms are used to describe camera scenes and other production elements.

3. Formats in which a video recording can be made include: interview, demonstration, documentary, and dramatization.

4. Planning a video recording involves selecting a title, analyzing the audience, writing objectives, outlining content, preparing a storyboard, and writing a script.

5. Making a video recording requires understanding the concept of motion, types of camera shots, and providing continuity.

6. Other important procedures include lighting scenes, preparing graphics, editing tapes, and caring for the camcorder.

7. Provide satisfactory viewing conditions for students.

Review Exercise

1. Match the terms on the left with explanations on the right.

___ a. Shot	1. Camera looking down at action
___ b. Medium shot	2. Camera appears to move in on action
___ c. High angle	3. Isolates important elements of subject
___ d. Scene	4. View showing specific details of subject
___ e. Long shot	5. Vertical camera movement
___ f. Low angle	6. Generally centers on action elements
___ g. Sequence	7. Camera looking up at action
___ h. Pan	8. Sets time and place for subject
___ i. Establishing shot	9. Horizontal camera movement
___ j. Tilt	10. Each time start button pushed and then released
___ k. Closeup shot	11. An event consisting of a number of shots
___ l. Zoom	

2. What are at least three styles in which a video recording for training can be made?

3. In planning a video recording, what two things should be done after title, audience, objectives, and content are specified?

4. To which production technique does each statement refer?
___ a. Set your feet in the direction toward which you will move the camera.
___ b. Matching the action in adjacent scenes.
___ c. Amount of time required for narration.
___ d. Key – Fill – Back.
___ e. Use this special lens effect sparingly.
___ f. Amount of time required by the action.
___ g. One scene leads logically to the next one.
___ h. Rearrange or shorten scenes.
___ i. Ratio of 4 to 3.
___ j. Maintain same screen direction from one action scene to the next one.

5. Which statements are TRUE with respect to camcorder and videotape care.
___ a. Videocassettes should be laid flat on a shelf when stored.
___ b. Keep video equipment away from electrical equipment that may generate magnetism.
___ c. Clean camera lens only with lens cleaning tissue.
___ d. Parts of video equipment exposed to dirt should be cleaned before use.
___ e. When the playback heads in the videoplayer are cleaned periodically, a good image will be seen on the screen.
___ f. Changes in temperature have little effect on video equipment.
___ g. Cap the camera lens when not in use.

Answers: 1. a – 10, b – 3, c – 1, d – 10, e – 6, f – 7, g – 11, h – 9, i – 8, j – 5, k – 4, l – 2.
    2. Interview, demonstration, documentary, dramatization.
    3. Draw a storyboard and write a script.
    4. a – pan, b – continuity, c – shot length, d – lighting, e – zoom, f – shot length,
       g – continuity, h – editing, i – titles and graphics, j – continuity.
    5. b,c,d,e,g.

References

"A Designer's Guide to Scriptwriting, Video Capabilities, and Limitations." P. E. Hunter. *Performance and Instruction,* 1990, *29*(3), 18-22.

Desktop Video. M. Wells. White Plains, NY: Knowledge Industry Publications, 1990.

Planning, Producing, and Using Instructional Technologies. J. E. Kemp and D C. Smellie. New York: HarperCollins, 1993.

"Scriptwriting: Write and Wrong." W. L. Hagerman. *Audio-Visual Communications, 30* (November 1986), 36-41; *30* (December 1986), 35-45; *31* (February 1987), 37-40.

Video Production Handbook. G. Millerson. Stoneham, MA: Focal Press, 1989.

Using Video: Interactive and Linear Designs. J. W. Arwady and D. M. Gayeski. Englewood Cliffs, NJ: Educational Technology Publications, 1989.

Video Users Handbook. P. Utz. White Plains, NY: Knowledge Industry Publications, 1989.

"Why Video is a Powerful Training Tool." L. Sneed. *Corporate Television, 7* (May/June 1989), 40-42.

Chapter 14

INTERACTIVE TECHNOLOGIES

In this chapter you will learn to:

- • **Recognize features of interactive media that make them useful for training.**
- • **Identify three forms of media that can be adapted for interactive learning and essential steps for their preparation.**
- • **Identify uses for computers, computer/video forms and multimedia in training, along with interactive program planning procedures.**
- • **Relate the use of interactive media within both classroom and the self-paced learning method of instruction.**

Media for instruction can be designed so that after a sequence of information is presented, the student is directed to answer one or more meaningful questions, make a decision or a choice, or take other action. Then, depending on the answer given, decision made, or the action taken, the student advances to another sequence of instruction or is directed to review the content already presented.

Interactive learning is the expression used to describe this interplay between student and instructional media. As opposed to passively observing a presentation, study with interactive media can result in active involvement for learning. The most effective use of interactivity is when a student studies with materials designed for flexible, self-paced learning as introduced on page 42.

Features

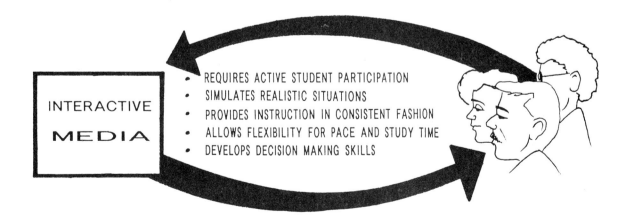

INTERACTIVE MEDIA

- • REQUIRES ACTIVE STUDENT PARTICIPATION
- • SIMULATES REALISTIC SITUATIONS
- • PROVIDES INSTRUCTION IN CONSISTENT FASHION
- • ALLOWS FLEXIBILITY FOR PACE AND STUDY TIME
- • DEVELOPS DECISION MAKING SKILLS

Forms of Interactive Learning Media

There are two categories of media for interactive learning:

- Adapting various forms of conventional media.
- Using computer-based technology (with or without controlling other media).

Interactive media apply many of the conditions and practices for successful learning described in Chapter 15. These components are found in most interactive technologies:

- Statement of learning objectives.
- Pretest for student preparation.
- Content divided into logical sections that require a reasonable amount of study time.
- Questions or exercises at the end of each section.
- Feedback on answers or actions of student.
- Self-check test for student to verify own learning.
- Posttest for determining student accomplishment of objectives.
- Review, retest, or advance to next instructional sequence.

With this approach, instruction could take place in the classroom. But, in many organizations, there is a growing necessity to provide more opportunities for employees to satisfy training requirements on their own, and at a time convenient to each person.

In the Introduction to this book on page xiii, this alternative to conventional training was indicated. Chapter 16 provides more detailed information as to how a flexible, self-instructional program can be developed and implemented. The use of interactive materials, as described here, can be the important resources in such a program.

Adapting Conventional Media

The three following examples describe how widely used instructional resources can be adapted for interactive learning.

Printed Material with Worksheets

If an instructional plan requires that students study a manual or other printed reference on their own, they can be guided with a set of worksheets. Here is the way it might be done:

1. Divide the subject content into manageable sections for study. This may be by text chapters or subject segments.
2. Write learning objectives for each section.
3. Develop participation activities for each segment, including review questions, exercises, problems, etc.
4. Provide answers and solutions for students.
5. Prepare a self-check test for each segment, or for the total program, so the student can verify learning.
6. Write instructions for students to proceed through the program, completing activities, and using the worksheets. (These would be given to students when they start to work.)
7. Have a colleague, or a few typical students, go over the instructional program to check for clarity and completeness.
8. Prepare instructor's posttest for the subject.

Audio Recording with Printed Material

Another approach to interaction is accomplished by preparing an audiotape recording that directs and guides students through the study of a topic. This can be a more personal method than using only printed materials with worksheets. Also, as with printed materials, these resources may be used at the convenience of, and, often at the location selected by, the individual student.

Refer to Chapter 12 for assistance in planning and preparing the audio recording. Follow this procedure for developing these resources:

1. Examine the content and divide it into sections.
2. Write learning objectives to be accomplished.
3. Decide how to:
   (a) introduce a section;
   (b) explain the content;
   (c) organize the planned recording so that the listener will be told when to stop the tape in order to refer to reading materials, diagrams, and so forth; then to restart it;
   (d) develop the participation activities with each section (questions, problems to solve, other activities in which to engage);
   (e) prepare answers for questions and problems.
4. Gather and prepare necessary written materials.
5. Prepare the script for the narration of each section, referring to all items under number 3 above. Remember this is *not* to be a lecture. A script segment may be from 2-3 minutes to possibly 10-12 minutes in length. The recording should be to clarify difficult or complex points, direct attention to the readings, learning activities, and exercises; then to provide feedback on answers with any necessary explanations.
6. Record the narration.
7. Check the recording and test the total program by having a colleague or a few students go through the program to be certain directions, explanations, and activities, with necessary materials, are clear and correct.
8. Duplicate the recording and written materials to provide the necessary number of copies for student use. Save the original audiotape recording as a master for future duplication.
9. Prepare the student self-test and the instructor's posttest.
10. Package the tape(s) and printed materials for student use.

Slide/Tape with Worksheet

Instructors using 35mm slides synchronized with an audiotape recording for instructional purposes will find it relatively easy to adapt the presentation for interactive learning. The slide program will need to be modified to include the features listed at the start of this chapter.

It will be necessary to add information slides that direct the student to stop the tape and answer questions listed on the worksheet. For immediate feedback, answers can be shown on the back or bottom of a worksheet page, or on the following slide. Also, you may want to use the slide medium to advantage by including new slides to show incorrect parts of a procedure that could be used in problem solving or testing. A new audio recording will have to be prepared.

The components of a slide/tape interactive program include:

1. Review learning objectives prepared for original slide/tape program.
2. Decide where the slide program should be divided into sections to permit

student interaction.

3. Develop questions, problems to solve, or other activity that should take place at the end of each section.
4. Prepare the worksheets and answers which will be part of the program.
5. Prepare information slides, which direct students to "stop the tape and refer to a section on the worksheet."
6. Modify the narration script to include student activities.
7. Re-record the narration and synchronize it with the slides (see Chapter 12).
8. Carry-out a test run with a colleague, or a few students, to be certain everything is ready for use.
9. Duplicate the slides, audio recording, and worksheets for student use, or if needed, transfer the program to videotape (see page 97).
10. Prepare posttest or other evaluations for subject.
11. Package the slide trays and printed materials for student use.
12. Decide where equipment (slide/tape equipment or videocassette/TV monitor) will be set up and available for student use.

Using Computer-Based Technologies

Computers are used extensively in every organization for recordkeeping, management, and in locating required information from database sources. In many vocational areas, microcomputers by themselves, or in combination with video, have become very useful in job skill training. Research evidence and practical experiences support these benefits for using computers in training:

- Efficient way to promote consistency of training throughout an organization.
- Can provide motivation to learning through both dynamic realism and an intellectual challenge with practical program materials.
- Persons with similar training needs can pair up to study together, thus sharing viewpoints and ideas.
- Gives students the flexibility to decide when and how long to study.
- Allows flexible study of only those sections of a program relevant to a student's learning needs.
- Efficient method of recordkeeping on student performance.
- Increased effectiveness in learning as compared with conventional methods.
- Can have positive cost benefits to the organization.

The use of interactive technologies can be successful for accomplishing the following training purposes:

- learning factual information;
- understanding generalizations;
- introducing physical skills;
- applying understandings and skills to practical job tasks;
- being prepared to handle practical situations and to solve job-related problems;
- developing positive attitudes toward work habits, co-workers, and other persons with whom technicians come in contact.

An increasing number of commercial computer software programs, video recordings, and videodiscs (including variations of the CD-ROM) are available for interactive technical training. Check with your local media library resources or a computer bookstore, and see the catalogs listed on page 69. If you want to develop your own computer-based interactive materials, the following sections of this chapter can serve as an introduction. For further details and specific uses with particular items of equipment, further assistance would be necessary. References listed at the end of the chapter can be helpful.

Essential Information

When any form of computer technology is to be developed for instruction, it is important to deal with the following:

Preliminary planning

Refer to the list of eight components on page 18 that are part of planning an interactive technology. As the development of the program proceeds, careful treatment of each component becomes necessary. The design of a computer-based instructional program can be a complex procedure, but the learning results can justify the efforts.

Linear and branching formats

The computer allows flexibility as to how a student can proceed through an interactive program. This differs from the previously described adaptations of conventional media. Those media forms require that an individual proceed in a **set order**, sequentially through the program. Each person sees, hears, and responds to the same content components. This is called a **linear format**.

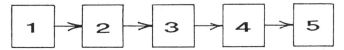

With a computer, while the linear format can be applied, it is possible to provide optional or branching paths for the student while moving through the program. A student with sufficient knowledge could follow a direct path, requiring few remedial loops. Another individual might choose, or be directed by the program, to review or receive further information if an exercise answer is incorrect. This **branching format** is one of the unique features of more sophisticated interactivity permitted by the computer.

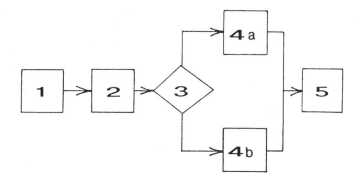

Various types of the branching pattern are common. Here are five formats of increasing complexity:

• Linear with repetition

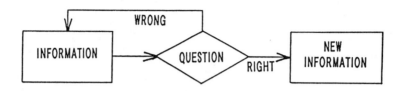

• Pretest and skip

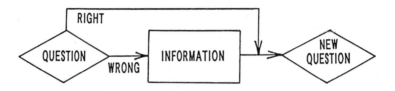

• Single remedial branch

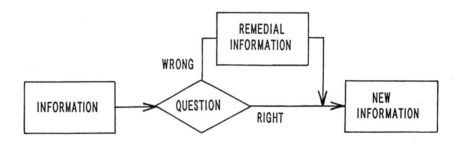

• Multiple remedial branch

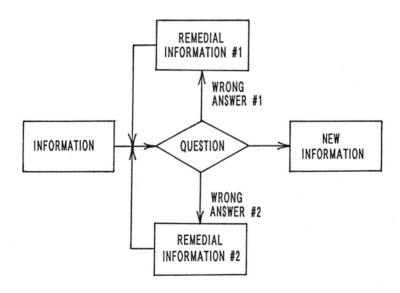

• **Compound branches**

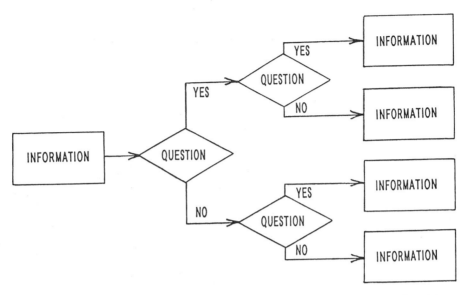

Each of these patterns might be used separately and repeatedly with content sequences, questions, and answers to form a complete instructional unit. Or, a variety of patterns might be considered to meet different learning objectives. A flowchart can help by visually planning the sequence elements within a branching pattern. This will illustrate how all elements of the program can be handled. Review information about flowcharting on page 15.

One procedure is to use the student's selected reply to a multiple choice review question for direction along different paths. As an example, this might be the treatment for one sequence of answers:

> **Reply 1**: Correct answer ... proceed to next program step.
> **Reply 2:** Incorrect answer ... try to answer question again.
> **Reply 3:** Incorrect answer ... receive further explanation,
>   then answer same or a new question.
> **Reply 4:** Incorrect answer ... be directed to lower level or
>   remedial information; be tested successfully before
>   returning to this question or similar one.

Authoring systems If you develop a computer-based training program of your own, you can instruct the computer with all details by using an **authoring system.** It requires no computer programming skill. By replying to a series of options or "prompts" presented as questions, you are guided to create a program with your own subject content.

Here is a typical set of prompts that could be used in an authoring system:

• What is the name of this lesson?
• Type the text and incorporate visuals to be displayed.
• State question number 1.
• Provide correct answer.
• How many tries are acceptable for a correct answer?

- What hint or other comment should be given after each wrong answer?
- Indicate expected incorrect answers.
- Provide feedback for expected wrong answers.
- Provide feedback for any unexpected answers.
- Do you have any questions that are unanswered?

Instead of being prompted by a set of verbal instructions or questions, **icons** can be used. They are small graphic images or symbols that clearly depict choices that can be activated as a person proceeds through a program.

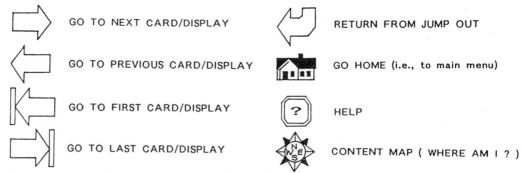

GO TO NEXT CARD/DISPLAY   RETURN FROM JUMP OUT

GO TO PREVIOUS CARD/DISPLAY   GO HOME (i.e., to main menu)

GO TO FIRST CARD/DISPLAY   HELP

GO TO LAST CARD/DISPLAY   CONTENT MAP (WHERE AM I ?)

Another interactive technique is to make a selection and click on a **button** which causes a certain action, on the screen, to take place.

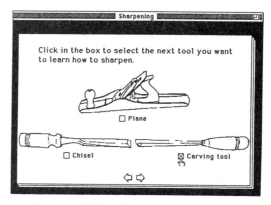

Source: Schwier and Misanchuk, *Interactive Multimedia Instruction.*
Reproduced with permission

Icon-based systems, like <u>Toolbook</u>, <u>Authorware Professional</u>, <u>Icon-Author</u> or <u>Tool Guide</u> are widely used for program authoring purposes with Macintosh and IBM-type computers.

Supporting software   In addition to authoring software, programs for word processing and graphics design can be used when preparing CBT. Preliminary materials are created with these programs and then "imported" through authoring tools into the CBT program.

Computer-Based Training (CBT)

Now build on the above information. With a software program, information is presented on the computer screen. This may consist of text, graphics, printed diagrams, photographs, and even computer-generated sound. Materials from other sources, like diagrams and photographs, can be "scanned" into computer memory by passing each item through a scanner attached to the computer.

Equipment   For using a scanner, the proper interface card will be needed for an expansion slot in the computer. Also, sufficient computer memory (at least 4 megabytes), suitable operating speed (with at least an 80386 or equal microprocessor), and a hard disk with at least 80 megabytes of storage should all be part of the computer.

Software   The best way to detail the information for each computer frame is to develop a storyboard illustration for each frame as indicated in the flowchart. (Software programs like *Canvas* for the Apple Macintosh and *MacroMedia Director* or *PC Paintbrush* for IBM-type computers are used for storyboarding computer frames.)

Screen design   When planning what will appear on a screen, follow these suggestions:

- Use short sentences for text and include only essential information (refer student to separate reading material and use voice output to reduce information on the screen).
- Use bold, simple lettering.
- Limit content to ten lines per screen and 25 characters per line.
- Use pastel color, like yellow, for words over dark (blue preferably) background.
- Maintain the flow of information from one screen image to the next.
- Appraise the continuity for all possible branches of the program.

Computer/Videotape

When subject content requires visual treatment with motion or the need to show complex relationships, then the video medium should be used with the computer. The computer provides directions, textual and graphics information, and manages the testing of learning. The video player presents visual segments, as directed by the computer. The two units function in coordination, rather than as separate entities.

Equipment   For an interactive videotape system, four or five pieces of equipment are required:

- Microcomputer with sufficient memory and operational speed.
- Videocassette player.
- A printed circuit board for interface that fits into an expansion slot in the computer.
- Computer connected to the videocassette player to locate segments on the tape and control tape movement.
- Video monitor(s) connected to the computer and videocassette player. The computer display screen can show both sets of images if a video overlay controller card is in the computer's system unit.

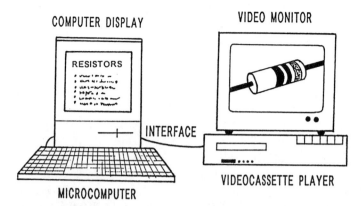

Video production

Review Chapter 13 on video production. A similar planning and production procedure as described previously would be applied when developing the video format. Preparing a script (page 107) and editing the tape recording require care, especially when the branching feature is used.

Programming the recording

When programming the recording, electronic signals must be put on the tape so the computer will locate specific start and stop points. This is done with a **control track** or a **time code** recorded on the tape. The computer reads the pulses or numbers and directs the videotape to play the segment accordingly.

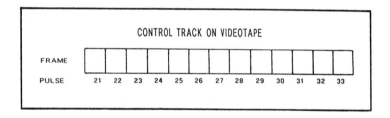

Using a barcode reader

An alternative to having the computer read code numbers, is to use **barcodes**. A barcode label is like the series of lines placed on a store product that is read by a scanner at the checkout counter. The label can be attached to a study guide page. It permits a person to locate exact points on a video recording. As a pen-like barcode reader is moved across the label, it reads the code for displaying a video segment. A software program locates exact start and stop points on the video.

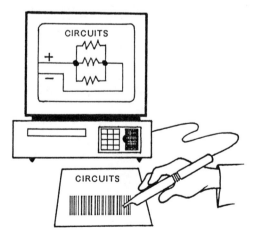

Computer/Videodisc

A video recording may be converted to a videodisc. It can contain a large amount of material, specifically, 54,000 still frames (words, diagrams, graphics, photos), 30 minutes of motion, or a combination of the two that is played by a laser stylus. Any still picture or motion sequence, in any order can be precisely accessed with one of the techniques described above.

Disc pro-duction

While a videotape recording can be produced in-house, the services for conversion to a videodisc are found usually in a qualified processing laboratory. After the master disc is made and checked for accuracy, multiple copies of the master disc are inexpensively prepared by the laboratory.

Instruct-ional use

The disc can be used by an instructor in a classroom. This requires only the videodisc player connected to a video screen. A manually operated remote control unit permits random access to program material on the disc. A barcode reader can be used as described above.

For individual students studying on their own, the videodisc player is interfaced with a computer. The player responds to commands from the computer and operates with fully programmed flexibility. Learning information and responding to simulated episodes can take place.

The realism of well-designed and visualized situations on a videodisc can motivate a student to think and make decisions. With such interactive materials, that can simulate real-life situations, a student can become actively involved in carrying out analysis, and problem solving relating to technical topics.

Other disc formats

Besides the standard 12 inch videodisc, there are other formats that use the same technology. Some recognized types are:

- CD-ROM (Compact Disc Read Only Memory) – can store up to 300,000 pages of text, graphics, photographs, and sound.
- CD-I (Compact Disc Interactive) – can store up to 8,000 high resolution still images, or up to 74 minutes of video and audio, in a CD-ROM format. Uses a stand-alone playback unit that contains a built-in computer chip for full interactive operation.
- DVI (Digital Video Interactive) – uses standard CD-ROM disc to store up to 72

minutes of full motion video and audio, or any combination of text (650,000 pages) and still media (40,000 images) forms.

Repurpos-ing There are many "generic" videodiscs available that contain general information on a subject that can be adapted for various instructional purposes. A disc may consist of a large collection of color slides, motion sequences, or a combination of both. For any essential skills or basic information, such a disc can be directly used or it can be **repurposed** (this means to use the disc for a different purpose than for which it was originally intended). Money required for planning and producing a new disc becomes unnecessary.

Examine the images on the disc. Develop a plan as described previously for any interactive program. Use an authoring system to program the visual images for the new use.

Interactive Multimedia

When various forms of media, including text, graphics, still pictures, voice, music, other sounds, animation, and full-motion video, are shown in various combinations, the term **multimedia** is used.   A computer program controls the order and arrangement of media components for use.

If the person using the program is able to choose what is to be shown, or makes decisions as directed, then meaningful interactive learning can take place. A program can include media material, providing branching paths, adjusting to the needs and interests of individual users, testing learning, and monitoring student progress.

HyperText The term **HyperText** refers to a series of pages or screens for a subject that can be viewed in any preferable arrangement. The user moves through a program by associating chunks (called "nodes") of information together through a chosen series of connections (called "links"). Two persons may use entirely different paths in their learning. Apple computer's **HyperCard** authoring software (for the Macintosh) is widely used to create many databases for this use.

HyperMedia When the HyperText concept is extended to linkage beyond just text material, to non-sequential multimedia forms, then the term **HyperMedia** applies. By clicking on a selected "button" on the computer screen, a "window" containing requested information is activated. As described above, this could result in the viewing of information through any type of media.

Many interactive multimedia resources are prepared as videodiscs, including the mentioned CD-ROM, CD-I, and DVI formats. Software programs such as *QuickTime* for Macintosh computers, *ToolBox* for IBM DOS computers, and *AmigaVision* for Amiga computers are used for multimedia materials.

Evaluating Interactive Programs for Use

When interactive media, either commercial or locally-produced programs, are considered for use, answer the following questions:

- Is the instructional manual (documentation) easy to use with clear directions for students?
- Are learning objectives specified?
- Is information presented accurate and up-to-date?
- Is the material free of racial, gender, or ethnic biases?
- Is material presented in an interesting, innovative way?
- Are text screens easy to read?
- Is the material free of grammatical, spelling, or other errors in language usage?
- Do graphics, color, and pictures contribute to understanding of content?
- Are frequent and sufficient exercises or other interactive activities provided?
- Is feedback immediate and clear?
- Does testing of learning directly indicate accomplishment of objectives?
- Do students, trying the program, attain mastery in a reasonable time?
- Is retesting available to trainees who require another opportunity to accomplish objectives?
- Can records of student performance easily be monitored?

Using Interactive Resources

While it is possible to use training materials designed for interactive learning as a regular classroom activity, they usually are more effective for **individual self-paced learning**. When you find application for this form of instructional media, review the discussion of self-paced learning in Chapter 5.

Be certain to prepare students for interactive study activities. They should understand the need for their active participation.

Be sure to provide a quiet area for the concentrated study that is required.

Summary

1. Interactive technologies can effectively apply the important conditions and practices that provide for successful learning.

2. The design of interactive media includes: objectives pretest, content sections, exercises, answers, test, review, and retest as necessary.

3. Instructional media that can be adapted for interactive learning include printed material/worksheets, audiotape recording/printed materials and worksheets, and slide/tape program with worksheets.

4. In addition to commercial software, locally produced programs for the computer and computer/video combination can provide for effective interactive learning.

> 5. When various forms of media are controlled by a computer or selected, in any sequence, by the student, then multimedia can be used for interactive learning.
>
> 6. A number of criteria can be used to judge the suitability of interactive materials when selection is being made.
>
> 7. While interactive media can be used in regular class activity, the best use is for self-paced learning.

Review Exercise

1. What is meant by the expression "interactive media"?

2. Why can forms of interactive media provide particularly effective training?

3. Within which teaching and learning method can interactive media be most successfully used?

4. Which of the following elements are included in the design of interactive media?

___ a. Pretest   ___ f . Program duplication
___ b. Exercises   ___ g. Feedback on answers
___ c. Tape editing   ___ h. Sequenced content
___ d. Learning objectives   ___ i . Sound recording
___ e. Review and retest   ___ j . Testing

5. What three types of media, or combinations of media, can be adapted to an interactive format?

6. Which items are advantages for using computers in training?
____ a. Can be excessively costly to an organization.
____ b. Provides consistent method of training for many persons.
____ c. Not flexible as all students must study same parts of a program.
____ d. Can allow for team learning as students study together.
____ e. Can contribute to increasing effectiveness of learning.
____ f . Useful mainly for learning facts with drilling methods.

7. Which statements are TRUE concerning computer-based training techniques?
____ a. When a videotape player is connected to a computer, a special circuit board is needed in the computer to control the interface function.
____ b. A videodisc can contain both still pictures and motion sequences.
____ c. Branching format programs are common in CBT interactive programs.
____ d. Videodiscs are designed for instructor use before a class, rather than for individual student use.

_____ e. One way to locate and direct the presentation of specific video segments is to use a barcode.

_____ f. Words on a computer screen should be preferably of dark lettering against a light colored background.

_____ g. A linear format program is developed with the help of a flowchart.

_____ h. To create a CBT interactive program, an authoring system is used.

_____ i. A computer screen image should be limited to ten lines of text.

_____ j. "Multimedia" refers to the capability of a computer to create and present all types of visual materials itself.

_____ k. "Repurposing" means that a computer program is developed for individual student use.

_____ l. All program components, including graphics and still pictures, need to be created with computer software.

_____ m. HyperMedia relates to viewing various media forms for a subject, according to an arrangement as called up by a student.

Answers: 1. Student required to respond, make a choice, or otherwise react as information is presented.
2. These forms of media apply many of the conditions and principles derived from psychology that are necessary for successful learning.
3. Self-paced learning.
4. a,b,d,e,g,h,j.
5. Print/worksheets, audiotape recording/ print and worksheets, slide/tape program/worksheets.
6. b,d,e.
7. a,b,c,e,h,i,m.

References

Developing Technical Training: A Structured Approach for the Development of Classroom and Computer-Based Instructional Materials. R. Clark. Reading, MA: Addison-Wesley, 1989.

"Interactive Design: Making Ideas into Multimedia." M. Magel. *AV Video,* 1991, *13*(5), 58-67.

The Educator's Handbook to Interactive Videodisc. E. Schwartz. Washington, DC: Association for Educational Communications and Technology, 1986.

Hypertext/Hypermedia. D. H. Jonassen. Englewood Cliffs, NJ: Educational Technology Publications, 1989.

Interactive Multimedia. D. Englebart and K. Hooper. Redmond, WA: Microsoft Press, 1988.

Interactive Multimedia Instruction. R. Schwier and E. R. Misanchuk. Englewood Cliffs, NJ: Educational Technology Publications, 1993.

Interactive Video. R. Schwier. Englewood Cliffs, NJ: Educational Technology Publications, 1987.

Making CBT Happen. G. Gery. Boston, MA: Weingarten Publications, 1987.

Planning, Producing, and Using Instructional Technologies. J. E. Kemp and D. C. Smellie. New York: HarperCollins, 1993.

"Software Tools for Interactive Media Developers." *Tech Trends,* 1991, *36*(2), 18-21.

"Text in Computer-Based Instruction: What the Research Says." M. G. Gillingham. *Journal of Computer-Based Instruction,* 1988, *15*(1), 1-6.

Using Video: Interactive and Linear Designs. J. W. Arwady and D. M. Gayeski. Englewood Cliffs, NJ: Educational Technology Publications, 1989.

Section C

PUTTING IT ALL TOGETHER

In the first section of this book the planning components for designing an instructional program received emphasis. While each element was treated separately, there is a close relationship among these components. This becomes apparent as you apply them to developing an instructional plan for the course and the topics that comprise it. This leads to the writing of lesson plans for each class period; developing media resources, self-instructional modules, or on-the-job training.

- DEVELOPING A COURSE PLAN
- SELECTING A TOPIC PLAN
- DESIGNING LESSON PLANS
- PREPARING LEARNING ENVIRONMENT
- DEVELOPING PRESENTATION SKILLS
- MEASURING TRAINING RESULTS

PLANS

TO ➡ TRAINING CENTER

In addition to making satisfactory arrangements for instruction within the classroom, instructors should examine their own classroom presentation skills. A number of suggestions are offered, while methods to diagnose and evaluate teaching styles are presented.

With increasing interest being given to student-centered training (see the Introduction), detailed information is provided on developing a plan for student self-instruction and for on-the-job training.

Finally, methods for gathering data to report results of an instructional program are examined. The success of training is determined by the effectiveness, efficiency, costs, reactions of students, and follow-up benefits.

This Section consists of four chapters:

Chapter 15. How Do I Develop an Instructional Plan, a Topic Plan, and a Lesson Plan?

Chapter 16. How Do I Develop and Implement a Flexible, Self-Instructional Plan and On-the-Job Training?

Chapter 17. How Do I Carry-out Classroom Instruction?

Chapter 18. How Do I Determine Training Results?

HOW DO I DEVELOP AN INSTRUCTIONAL PLAN, A TOPIC PLAN, and A LESSON PLAN?

In this chapter you will learn to:

> * Recognize conditions for successful learning.
> * Design an overall instructional plan for a course.
> * Develop a plan for each topic.
> * Develop a lesson plan for a class meeting.
> * Sequence subject content in four ways.

Principles and Practices for Successful Learning

Throughout this book it has been emphasized that the purpose of instruction is to facilitate learning. In its simplest terms, we can say that learning is "what goes on in the student's head." This require memorizing, understanding, applying information, carrying-out tasks, and accomplishing other learning outcomes.

As you organize the various planning elements presented in Part A of this book, make use of what is known about learning psychology. For learning to be most successful, a number of accepted principles and practical experiences should be applied as plans are developed.

Prelearning Preparation   Students should have satisfactorily achieved a level that is necessary before starting present training. If students do not have the necessary background preparation, their training may not be successful.

Learning Objectives   Successful learning is more likely when students are informed of the specific objectives to be achieved.

Organization of Content   Learning can be improved when content and procedures are organized into meaningful sequences. The size of each segment, as presented to students, depends on logical divisions, complexity, and difficulty.

Processing Information   Present new information in a meaningful order and in manageable "chunks" at one time (up to **seven** bits — facts, explanations, steps in a procedure), for students to learn during a single study interval. Then by combining chunks, reviewing, and using the information, it can pass to permanent learning.

Individual Differences   Students learn at different rates and in different ways. Therefore, a variety of instructional procedures, within groups and by individuals, should be considered.

Motivation A person must be motivated to want to learn. Motivation can be stimulated by:
- making it apparent that what is to be learned is important and useful;
- providing a variety of learning experiences;
- recognizing successful learning which encourages further learning efforts.

Training Resources When instructional resources, including forms of simple and sophisticated media, are carefully selected and integrated to support learning activities, a significant impact on student achievement can result.

Participation Active participation by students is preferable to lengthy periods of passive listening and viewing in a classroom.

Feedback Motivation for learning can be continued or increased when students are informed of their progress. Feedback confirms correct understandings and performance, provides knowledge of mistakes, and remedies faulty learning. For satisfactory learning, there is a close connection between feedback and reinforcement.

Reinforcement Learning motivated by success through feedback is rewarding and builds confidence. Thus, student efforts are reinforced to continue learning.

Practice and Repetition To ensure that the results of learning will be retained for a long period of time, provision should be made for students to review the information or practice the skill as soon as possible after instruction.

Application Provide opportunities for students to apply new learning to a variety of realistic tasks.

Instructor's Attitude A positive attitude shown by the instructor can influence motivation and attitudes of students. Personal enthusiasm for teaching, consideration of students, and expressed interest, along with competence in the subject, are ways to do this.

You have seen reference to many of these principles and practices in previous chapters of this book. As you develop lesson plans and decide on training activities, make use of this list.

Organize the Training Course

In the first section of this book you were introduced to the seven essential components for a good training plan:

- Assessing instructional needs
- Content outline and skill procedures for a topic
- Learning objectives
- Student characteristics
- Instructional methods
- Instructional resources
- Testing for learning

You should now be ready to organize these components to develop specific plans for your teaching. These consist of three major steps:

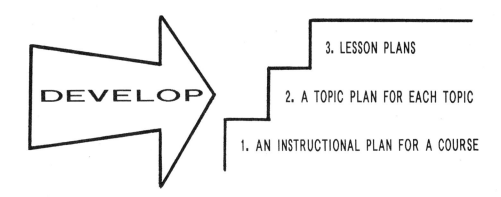

Instructional Plan for a Course

If you are responsible for an instructional program that will include a number of topics for a subject extending over a number of class sessions, then it is important to design an overall plan.

Here is an outline, with questions to help in preparing such a plan:

1. **Subject for Course**
   - What is the subject?

2. **Goal** (see page 11)
   - What training goal is to be accomplished?

3. **Topics** (see page 12)
   - What topics will comprise the course?

4. **Anticipated number of students**
   - How many students will be trained?

5. **Prerequisites** (see page 33)
   - What basic abilities, background knowledge, or skills should the students have acquired before starting the course?

6. **Potential Activities** (see Chapter 5)
   - What training and learning activities from the categories of presentation, self-paced learning, and group work, would be appropriate?

7. **Resources** (Chapter 6 and Section B, Chapters 8-14)
   - Are there specific media or other resources available for use?
   - What other resources should be obtained or prepared?

8. **Facilities**
   - What classroom, study area, or other facility will be required or available?

9. **Schedule**
   - When will instruction start?
   - What will be the length of the course?
   - What will be the daily or weekly schedule?

10. **Testing** (Chapter 7)
    - What testing methods will be used to measure learning?

11. **Expectations** (page 164)
    - What level of proficiency will be required for students?

Here is an example of how the above questions can be answered:

Subject: Industrial Robotics
Topics: Background and Scope
       Configurations
       Control Systems
       End Effectors and Workhandling
       Sensors and Sensory Feedback
       Programming
       Safety Considerations
       Applications
Goal: To provide an introduction and overview of robotic technology as applied to manufacturing industries
Number of students: 30-40
Prerequisites: Knowledge of: Physical mechanics
                       Basic electronics
                       Computer fundamentals
Potential activities: Instructor presentations
                  Demonstrations
                  Individual study
                  Lab for teams and individuals
Resources: Robotic equipment
          Text — *Elements of Industrial Robotics*
         Student study guide with readings, worksheets, diagrams, photos,
         Video recording — *Introduction to Robotics*
Facilities: Classroom
        Robotic laboratory
        Self-instruction lab with video equipment
Schedule: Course: October 2 – December 15
        Classroom 2 — 2 hour sessions per week
        Lab 2– 4 hour sessions per week
        Self-paced learning lab open 20 hours per week
Testing: Objective written tests
       Practical skills in lab
       Project completion
Expectations: 85% learning proficiency for 90% of students

The above eleven elements comprise a practical framework for an instructional course. Next, develop each topic in the course.

Topic Plan

Each topic that is listed under the course plan can be developed according to the following outline and questions:

1. **Questions** (page 13)
   - What questions should students be able to answer as the result of instruction on the topic?

2. **Subject Content/Skills** (Chapter 2)
   - What subject content and performance skills should be learned in answer to the questions?

3. **Learning Objectives** (Chapter 3)
   - With what learning objectives for the topic should students become competent?

4. **Pretest** (page 33)
   - What prerequisites should students have acquired before starting this topic?
   - Should students be pretested on content for the topic?

For each topic, by satisfactorily answering the questions for these four planning elements, you will then be prepared for writing lesson plans.

Here is an example of a Topic Plan:

Topic: Robot Use Safety Considerations

Questions: 1. What are five potential hazard situations within a robot installation?
2. What five techniques can be used to prevent direct injury to humans?
3. How can three potential causes for injury during operation be avoided?
4. In the case of hardware failure or malfunction, what precautions can be taken to avoid injury?
5. How can you prevent a control system failure or malfunction?

Content/Skill:
A. Hazard situations
   1. Human failings, acts, or omissions
   2. Robot operation
   3. Hardware or operation failure
   4. Control system failure or malfunction
   5. Malfunction of external sensors, equipment, and safety devices
B. Prevent human injury
   1. Physical guarding and fencing
   2. Monitoring to prevent unauthorized access
   3. Safety control devices
   4. Safe working system
   5. Training and familiarization of personnel
C. Safe robot operation

   ....

D. Avoid dangers from potential hardware failure

   ....

E. Avoid control system failure and malfunction

   ....

Learning Objectives: (100% competence with each objective)
1. To recognize five potential hazard situations with robotic installation
2. To access five techniques to prevent injury to humans
3. To analyze how three potential causes of injury can be avoided during robot operation
4. To recall three potential causes for hardware failure
5. To explain five ways that hardware failure can be avoided
6. To describe two ways that control system failure can be avoided

Pretest:
1. Which type of movement configuration is described? (prerequisite from topic #2)
   a. Three axes at right angles
   b. Combining both vertical and horizontal linear movement
   c. Single linear motion with two perpendicular rotary movements
2. Describe three working configurations. (prerequisite from topic #2)
3. List four potential hazards with a robot installation. (topic pretest)
4. What would you do to avoid a control system failure? (topic pretest)
   (Trainees who grade 100% on Pretest can request special project activity instead of attending two hour class session on topic.)

Lesson Plan

For each session in a conventional course (or a single class period that comprises an instructional program), a plan or schedule should be prepared. This is known as a **training schedule** or more commonly, a **lesson plan**. The plan would guide activities for the instructor and students. Keep in mind that there may be regulations and procedures established by your organization or department that you should follow in your lesson planning.

There are various forms that a lesson plan can take. Following is a suggested outline:

1. Introduce Topic
- How are students to be made aware of the importance or value of the topic? (Where and how it is used; consequences of use.)
- Does the topic relate to previous or forthcoming lessons?
- When should students be informed of the objectives for the topic? (Chapter 3)
- Are all students adequately prepared for the topic? (Pretest, page 33)

2. Present Information/Skill Procedures
- What subject content or procedures relate to the objectives? (Chapter 2)
- How will the content be segmented and sequenced?
  (See examples of sequencing that follow on page 141.)
- What examples or illustrations can be used to explain content?
- What instructional procedures can be used to accomplish each group of objectives? (Chapter 5)
- What specific resources will be used for each segment of instruction? (Chapter 6)
- What time allocations can be set for each activity?

3. Provide for Student Participation/Practice/Applications
- What activities will involve trainees? (page 41)
- What materials are needed for students?

4. Review
- How can the content presented be summarized?
- How can any unanswered questions or unclear concepts be remedied?

5. Test Learning
- How is student competency with the objectives measured? (Chapter 7)
- When should testing take place?

As you develop the teaching and learning activities for each lesson period, be sure to refer to the principles and practices of learning outlined at the beginning of this chapter. Also consider the methods for sequencing content that follow. Develop the plan in a diagram as shown in the example on page 142.

Sequencing Content

The question — **How will the content be segmented and sequenced?** — has been indicated as important in lesson planning. When we considered the selection and outlining of subject content in Chapter 2 on page 12, three levels of content were considered:

(1) facts, terms, definitions
(2) descriptions, functions, processes
(3) concepts, rules, principles, regulations, codes

Use the above categories to decide how to sequence the content. Here are ways it can be done:

- **Whole-to-Part:** Start with an overview of the complete topic, then refer to each section, part, or element of procedure. Students can see how each part relates to the whole. This is known as a **deductive** approach to training.

  Example –

  > **Topic**: Making plastic film for packaging
  >   1. **Overview:** The process for making plastic films for packaging requires the transformation of solid polymer resins from granular form into film on rolls.
  >   2. **Part:** Explain extrusion process (polymer feeding, melting, mixing, filtration).
  >   3. **Part:** Film-making sequence (melted film formation, quenching, windup).

- **Part-to-Whole**: Examine each section, part, or element of procedure for the topic. Build to an understanding of the complete subject or operation. This is known as an **inductive** approach to training.

  Example –

  > **Topic**: Package functions
  >   1. **Part:** Introduce factors of dirt, dust, rain; atmospheric gases; loss of flavor/odor; effect of light; temperature extremes; insect infestation; tampering and pilfering.
  >   2. **Whole:** Take all above into account for preserving/protecting a product.

Training Schedule / Lesson Plan

Content Headings (from Topic Plan)	Instructor (What to do)	Students (Activities)	Resources (use in Class)	Time
Introduction	Show video segment "Robot Safety Problems" Discuss what went wrong; how could be prevented	Watch video Discuss	Video #18, segment 1 VCR/TV receivers	20 min.
	Refer to Topic objectives	See list Objectives	Study guide page 88	
	Refer to Pretest results	Review prerequisites	Text	
A. Hazard Situations	Describe situations Demonstrate on robot	Take notes Reply to worksheet questions	Overhead transparencies Study guide page 89 Demo robot	15 min.
B. Ways to prevent injury during operation	Indicate features and practices on demo robot	Take notes Answer questions Complete diagram Examine robot environment	Study guide pages 91-95 Demo robot	20 min.
----- Break -----				
C. Safe robot operation	Show video segment "Safe Robot Operation" Stop at each manipulation and discuss	Watch video Discuss Complete worksheet	Video #18, segment 2 VCR/TV receivers Study guide pages 97-100	30 min.
D. Hardware failure	Prepare for lab	Listen to instructions	Activity sheets and readings	20 min.
E. Control system failure	Handout team activity problems and readings Summarize A,B,C sections as necessary	Meet as team to plan Raise questions Follow summary		

(Lab session follows. Test topic objectives at start of next class period. Announce to class.)

- **Known-to-Unknown**: Start by referring to what students already know about the topic and gradually introduce new information or procedures.

Example –

> **Topic:** Molecular structure of plastic material
> 1. **Known:** C-carbon, H-hydrogen, Cl-chlorine; CH_2 or (monomer units)
>
> 2. **New:** $C-C-C-C-C-C-$ Polymer (formed by $H-H-H-H-H$ polymerization)
>
> 3. **New:** Chemical action to replace some H ions with Cl ions to form polyvinyl chloride (a plastic material)

- **Step-by-Step**: Treat a procedure or task by presenting the steps in a logical, operational, or time-required order.

Example –

> **Topic:** Operation of plastic bag making and filling machine
> (1) Film drawn into machine
> (2) Film folded
> (3) Two sides of film sealed
> (4) Bag cut from advancing plastic web
> (5) Fill product into open mouth of bag
> (6) Seal bag along top

Summary

1. Principles derived from learning theory and practical experience that contribute to successful teaching and learning include: prelearning, objectives, content organization, processing information, individual differences, motivation, resources, participation, feedback, reinforcement, practice and repetition, application, and trainer's attitude.

2. An instructional plan consists of eleven elements: subject, topics, goal, number of students, prerequisites, potential activities, resources, facility, schedule, testing, and expectations.

3. A topic plan consists of four elements: questions, objectives, subject content/skills, and pretest.

4. A lesson plan includes five elements: introduction of topic, presentation of information/skill, provision for participation/

> practice, reviewing and summarizing, and testing of learning.
>
> 5. Subject content can be sequenced from whole-to-part, from part-to-whole, from know-to-unknown, or in step-by-step order.
>
> 6. A form is useful for specifying all elements of a lesson plan with headings: content, activities (instructor/students), resources, and time.

Review Exercise

1. Following are applications of the principles and practices of learning described in this chapter. Before each one write the most appropriate principle it represents.

____ a. Selecting CBT as a media form for learning about a topic.

____ b. Providing students with a copy of the outcomes they are to accomplish for a topic.

____ c. Making the answers to problems available to students immediately after they complete their work.

____ d. Influencing students in class by instructor's tone of voice and visible manner toward the subject.

____ e. Having students complete a worksheet as they listen to a lecture.

____ f . Allowing students to progress through a unit at their own study pace.

____ g. Giving a test covering content a student should already know before starting a new topic.

____ h. Giving students a number of opportunities to perform the manipulations required in the skill development.

____ i . Having students solve new problems relating to the content just studied.

____ j. Allowing students to check their own learning by completing self-check tests; by getting correct answers, student sees positive progress.

____ k. Dividing content for a topic into small sections, with participation activity for each section before starting next section.

____ l . Showing a video recording as an introduction for a new topic.

____ m. Presenting students with five of a total of nine items of information, reviewing them in worksheets, then introducing the remaining four items.

2. Following are some details for planning training on the subject of *Automotive Maintenance and Repair*. Place each item within one of these categories — **Training Plan, Topic Plan,** or **Lesson Plan.**

____ a. Questions: What are the six parts of a fuel system?
                 How is vapor lock overcome?

____ b. Use demonstration technique.

____ c. Training starts May 5; consists of 6 two-hour sessions.

____ d. Read manual section on fuel system.

____ e. Decide on time to be devoted to practice for each activity.

____ f . Topics: Fuel systems
        Cooling system
        Brakes
        Steering and suspension

____ g. Components of fuel system
        a. fuel tank   d. fuel filter
        b. fuel line   e. carburetor or fuel injection
        c. fuel pump   f. air cleaner

____ h. Demonstrate way to overcome vapor lock.

____ i . Automotive technicians who have completed apprentice program.

____ j . Student replaces fuel filter.

____ k. Objectives: To test a fuel injection system for proper operation
                To locate six components of a fuel system accurately
                To eliminate a vapor lock completely

____ l . Provide 4 different engines for lab use.

3. To which method of sequencing content does each example apply?
    a. Robot startup procedure
        (1) Remove unnecessary items in working area
        (2) Ensure that end effector does not hold a component
        (3) Take note of position of fixtures and any obstructions
        (4) Check all connections to robot for secure operation
        (5) Check robot mounts
    b. Fundamental elements: source of illumination, camera system, computer interface, software
      Process: image capture, digitizing, data analysis
      Result: robot vision to detect presence, position and movement of objects
    c. (1) In everyday arithmetic we use Arabic numbers with digits 0-9.
       (2) A *binary* number system consists of just two digits 0 and 1. This becomes the electronic digital system used to communicate in computers and audio equipment.
    d. (1) The movement of the robot arm requires control of axis movement, position, and velocity.
       (2) To accomplish this, nine elements are necessary. They are: actuator, manipulator, control system, control software, end effector, etc.

Answers: 1. a – resource, b – objectives, c – feedback, d – instructor attitude,
        e – participation, f – individual differences, g – prelearning, h – practice,
        i – application, j – reinforcement, k – content organization, l – motivation,
        m– processing information.
    2. Training plan – b,c,f,j. Topic plan – a,g,l. Lesson plan – d,e,h,i,k,m.
    3. a – Step-by-Step; b – Part-to-Whole; c – Known-to-Unknown; d – Whole-to-Part.

References

"Building a Lesson Plan." D. Torrence. *Training and Development Journal,* 1987, *41*(5), 91-95.

"A Comparison of Two Formats for an Instructor's Guide." D. McLinden, O. Cummings, and S. Bond. *Performance Improvement Quarterly,* 1990, *3*(1), 2-13.

"Curriculum Planning for Training: The State of the Art." W. Rothwell and H. Kazanas. *Performance Improvement Quarterly,* 1988, *1*(3), 2-16.

Designing Effective Instruction and Learning. J. E. Kemp, G. M. Morrison, and S. M. Ross. Columbus, OH: Macmillan, 1993.

Designing Training Programs: The Critical Events Model. L. Nadler. Reading, MA: Addison-Wesley, 1982.

Enhancing Adult Motivation to Learn: A Guide to Improving Instruction and Increasing Learner Achievement. R. Wlodkowski. San Francisco: Jossey-Bass, 1985.

Essentials of Learning for Instruction. R. M. Gagne and M. P. Driscoll. Englewood Cliffs, NJ: Prentice-Hall, 1988.

I. D. Project Management. M. D. Greer. Englewood Cliffs, NJ: Educational Technology Publications, 1992.

Instructional Design: Principles and Applications. L. J. Briggs, K. L. Gustafson, and M. H. Tillman, eds. Englewood Cliffs, NJ: Educational Technology Publications, 1991.

Making Instruction Work. R. F. Mager. Atlanta, GA: Center for Effective Performance, 1990.

"Ten Principles of Learning Revised in Accordance with Cognitive Psychology: With Implications for Teaching." S. F. Foster. *Educational Psychologist,* 1986, *21*(3), 235-243.

Thirty-Five Lesson Formats: A Sourcebook of Instructional Alternatives. P. Lyons. Englewood Cliffs, NJ: Educational Technology Publications, 1992.

"Strategies for Stimulating the Motivation to Learn." J. M. Keller. *Performance and Instruction,* 1987, *26*(8), 1-7.

Chapter 16

HOW DO I DEVELOP AND IMPLEMENT A FLEXIBLE, SELF-INSTRUCTIONAL PLAN and ON-THE-JOB TRAINING?

In this chapter you will learn to:

> • **Recognize benefits and limitations of a self-instructional program.**
> • **Review eight components necessary for preparing a self-study module.**
> • **Identify ten components of a module.**
> • **Plan actions under three headings when preparing to use a module.**
> • **Consider at least twelve factors for evaluating the use of a module.**
> • **Plan on-the-job training.**
> • **Evaluate on-the-job training.**

For effective training, apply:

- the principles and practices for successful learning listed on page 135;
- information about student preparation for training and their learning styles (Chapter 4);
- adult learning features (page 34);

then consider designing a learner-centered, interactive, self-paced program. This would allow each student to progress through the training at a preferred pace, within the time schedule you set. The structure of the program can guide the student to reach the competency levels you establish.

Benefits and Limitations of a Self-Instructional Program

Many organizations are active in improving products and services by applying *Total Quality Management* (TQM) practices within phases of their operation. A systematically developed, flexible learning program can be considered as a **total quality approach** to training.

Benefits   The advantages for this method of training include:

- Can be better related to student needs than can conventional, classroom instruction.
- Instructor becomes a guide, and learning manager, rather than simply a dispenser of information.
- A flexible approach since students can decide, in consultation with the instructor or supervisor (or for themselves), which units to study and in what order, thus assuming greater responsibility for their own learning.
- Individuals can manage their own learning and may apply the practices in future independent study.
- Students can set their own schedule and possibly select convenient location for study.
- Can be a cost-effective method when serving large numbers of students.

Limitations   Following are limitations when this approach to training is used:

- Some students are not comfortable with this method. They feel isolated, and prefer training in a class or group mode.
- Not feasible if information or procedures to be learned must be changed frequently.
- Requires more effort and expense to develop and prepare self-study packages and accompanying resources.
- Unless deadlines are set, some individuals lack the discipline to apply themselves and may delay in completing assignments.

Developing a Self-Study Module

For this training method, subject matter needs to be organized into one or more self-study units. These are often called **modules** (or packages). As you learned on page 12, a subject usually can be divided into a number of topics. Each topic, or subtopic for a complex topic, could become a separate module.

Preparation   In preparing to develop self-study modules, review the following pages and chapters of this book:

- Self-paced learning advantages, limitations, and applications (page 42)
- Learning principles and practices (page 135)
- Media resources and media selection procedure (Chapter 6)
- Interactive technologies, both conventional and computer-based (Chapter 14)

In addition to the above, be prepared to apply the components of planning treated in Part A of the book:

- Subject content and performance skills (Chapter 2)
- Learning objectives (Chapter 3)
- Pretesting (page 33)
- Testing learning (Chapter 7)

Once you have specified the learning objectives in terms of the content and skills for a topic, select the media that will be part of each module. These materials may:

- already be available for direct use;
- have to be adapted for interactive learning (Chapter 4);
- need to be prepared (Chapters in Part B).

If instruction is to take place off-worksite, these resources may be useful:

- Student-instructor direct contact via the telephone.
- Verbal messages sent via electronic mail service.
- Student-prepared work sent to instructor (and possibly to other students) via fax transmission.
- Communication between instructor and student via computer with connected modem.
- Combinations of the above.

Contents   The package should consist of a printed study guide and accompanying media materials or instructions for acquiring the media needed. A computer-based training program may contain the elements of the study guide as part of the software.

The study guide should include:

1. Module title.
2. Goal for module.
3. Carefully stated directions for using the package.
4. Pretest to determine student's preparation and possible competence with part or all of the module content. A successful grade, as specified by the instructor, would allow a student to bypass studying part or all of the module.
5. Directions for how to overcome any deficiencies in preparation.
6. Learning objectives to be accomplished.
7. List of resources for use while studying.
8. Description of learning activities and resources (possibly with alternative choices so student can select a preferred way of study) relating to each objective or set of objectives.
9. Exercises relating to each activity with feedback on responses.
10. Self-check tests of learning, with answers, to enable students to evaluate their own progress.
11. Posttest for instructor evaluation of learning, with review, restudy, and retesting if necessary for student to reach mastery.
12. Follow-up activities and applications for individual or groups of students.

Example of self-instructional module content –
    (Only a sampling of each element is included.)

Title: Plastic Packaging Machinery
Goal: To understand how a variety of food and beverage packaging systems can be used
Directions: Complete pretest and check answers.
    Study the activities necessary to accomplish objectives.
    Complete exercises and check answers.
    Self-test yourself with self-check test.
    When ready, request posttest.
    Complete follow-up lab work.
Pretest: 1. In packaging, besides a high quality product, what additional requirement is essential? (prerequisite knowledge)
    2. List the stages of food and beverage processing for packaging. (Objective #1)
    3. What are two categories of filling systems? (Objective #2)
    4. Describe the operational steps of a vertical form-fill-seal machine. (Objective #3)
(Answers available)
For questions incorrectly answered —
    Prerequisite — Review Chapter 1 in book *Packaging Foods with Plastic.*
    Other questions — study module activities per objective

Learning Objectives:
1. To identify the three stages in food and beverage packaging
2. To compare differences between the filling process for liquids and for dry products
3. To differentiate classes of pouch sealing from use of closures
4. To describe three methods for imprinting labels
5. To judge final package integrity

Resources: Reference — *Packaging Foods With Plastics* by Jenkins and Harrington
Video #12 — *Packaging Foods*
Equipment — Vertical form-fill-seal machine
Horizontal form-fill-seal machine
Pouch machine
Materials — Sample closures
Plastic films

Activities:
Objective #1: Examine diagram of food and beverage processing and packaging systems on p. 67. Study stages in system.
1. What are the three systems illustrated?
2. To which stage does each apply?
   a. plugs   d. piston with value
   b. offset   e. flat bottom bag
   c. gravity flow   f. 3-sided pouch
Answers ....

Objective #2: Read Filling Systems, pages 69-88.
View Part 1 of video #12 — *Methods for Filling Containers.*
1. Liquid packaging involves volumetric filling by means of _____.
2. Draw diagrams showing how two piston volumetric filling units operate.
3. What are three ways for filling dry products?
Answers ....

Posttest: Examine the vertical and horizontal filling and sealing machines. Note numbers on parts. Which machine or location relates to the following?
1. Filling system for each machine
2. Sealing system for each machine
3. Labeling system for each machine
4. Timed flow filling unit
5. Diaphram volumetric filling unit

Follow-up activity: Preparation for lab work with filling machines

Using a Self-Study Module

The following checklist should be followed when using a self-study module:

1. Orient students to use of module
   - Place to study (possibly close to work area or at location chosen by student)
   - Set-up and operation of equipment for using module resources
   - Deadline for successful module completion
   - Available assistance
   - Start with completion of pretest

2. Instructor responsibilities
   - Review pretest results with student and advise preparatory work necessary or parts of module to study
   - Be available at appropriate times for consultation
   - Monitor student progress
   - Administer module posttest
   - Keep record on module completion
   - Arrange and handle follow-up activities

3. Plan to maintain records of student work (on paper or in computer file)
   - Name of student (or assigned file number)
   - Module title or number
   - Starting date
   - Pretest results
   - Posttest results
   - Completion date
   - Remarks (difficulties encountered, special assistance requested, time for completion, etc.)

Evaluating Self-Study Modules

When a self-study module is developed, it should be tested with two to three students representative of the group which will use it. Judge the results. Revise parts of the program as necessary.

You may want to develop a checklist or a series of rating scale items (page 167) for gathering student reactions to use of a module:

- Are students able to follow directions easily and move smoothly through the activities and self-check tests?
- Does the pretest accurately reveal student deficiencies in preparation?
- Are recommended remedial activities satisfactory for overcoming deficiencies?
- Are students able to skip ahead without confusion if they already show competence with part of the topic?
- Is the sequence within the module clear and logical to the student?
- Are suitable activities included that treat each objective?
- Is the reading level satisfactory for ease of understanding, without talking down to a student?
- Is adequate space provided for response to questions?
- Are low-level information and skills used to provide higher-order learning experiences and practical applications?

- Are suitable options provided for students to select resources they prefer to use?
- Is a student able to check progress while proceeding through activities?
- Are follow-up activities provided to apply the learning on the job?
- Is the study time required by a student reasonable (1-3 hours)?

If CBT (computer-based training) or other interactive materials are used in a module, refer to the evaluation criteria listed on page 129.

Developing On-the-Job Training

OJT (on-the-job training) can be a widely used, effective method for technical training. On page 47 this technique was introduced. Instructional situations appropriate for OJT include:

- Limited number of employees require training
- Employees to be trained on-site, rather than elsewhere
- Required competence with newly acquired equipment
- Procedural changes to meet new safety needs

There are two forms of OJT. In the **unstructured** approach, an employee "picks up" job responsibilities and task procedures in a casual, often haphazard way from another employee. When a specific training plan is developed and implemented, it becomes a **structured** OJT plan. The following benefits can result from a structured OJT program:

- Training relates immediately to job assignment
- Mastery of tasks to be learned can be guaranteed
- Experienced employees can be recognized as trainers
- Supervisors and new employees can become better acquainted
- Respect among co-workers can be enhanced

Guidelines   The following guidelines should be applied in developing OJT:

1. Make sure the student or employee understands the importance and purpose of the task to be learned.

2. Provide a list of learning objectives (with required performance standards) to be accomplished.

3. Develop one or more job aids (page 43) for training use. Common ones are:
   - a procedure list or activities checklist
   - a trouble-shooting table
   - a decision guide
   - diagrams or photographs
   - safety warnings

4. Recognize student behaviors within three stages of learning:
   - Stage 1: Immediately after demonstration and study, response to task performance is slow, many mistakes are made.
   - Stage 2: With practice errors are reduced, response time is still moderately slow.
   - Stage 3: With additional practice error rate reaches zero, with response

time faster and the individual attains a satisfactory performance level.

5. Conclude training when evaluation of learning shows employee has satisfactorily attained the objectives.

6. OJT may not be suitable if:
   • the workplace is very noisy
   • the use of specialized equipment could disrupt normal production
   • hazardous materials to be handled could put the untrained employee at risk

Plan, Use, Evaluate OJT

The details for planning, implementing, and evaluating OJT are listed below:

1. Instructor Preliminary Planning
   • State the goal to be accomplished (page 11).
   • Analyze procedures and skills required (page 14).
   • Develop knowledge outline and procedural lists or flowchart for skill (Chapter 2).
   • Specify and sequence learning objectives with required performance standards and conditions (Chapter 3).
   • Obtain or prepare job aids, printed materials, or other resources (Chapter 6 and Chapters in Part B).
   • Decide on necessary preparatory knowledge or hands-on experience employee should already have (page 33).
   • Develop a checklist, rating scale, or other proficiency measures, as well as written questions to determine employee competence after training (Chapter 7).
   • Carry-out the actual task to be performed as a review of procedural details and use of equipment.
   • Decide approximate training time required and set schedule for employees.

2. Instructor Preparation
   • Arrange for training site.
   • Set out materials, tools, and equipment.
   • Provide manuals, job aids, and other media or reference materials.
   • Consider safety precautions and procedures.

3. Student Preparation
   • Take prerequisite/pretest (including English, math, dexterity skills).
   • Complete remedial study as necessary.
   • Complete pretest to determine competency level with subject.
   • Review written reference materials or media (often video) for study before training.

4. Training session
   • Instructor explains goal and importance of task to job.
   • Instructor reviews learning objectives.
   • Instructor describes procedure and equipment use, including cautions, safety practices, and care of equipment.
   • Instructor demonstrates skill initially at normal pace, then repeats at slower pace while talking through details and answering questions from

employee. (Note seven "chunk" limitation for information processing on page 135.)
- Employee tries out task, verbally describing steps in task while proceeding, using job aids and references; being coached and corrected by instructor.
- Employee practices skills until proficiency is reached.

5. Evaluate learning and certify competence
- Instructor prepares area, materials, and equipment for testing.
- Instructor administers written test for knowledge as necessary.
- Instructor tests employee performance skills, using checklist and rating scale, making observation notes for evaluation.
- Instructor reviews testing results with employee.
- When competence is reached, instructor certifies completion of training in personnel record. If appropriate, awards certificate to employee.
- Without acceptable competence, instructor provides for employee retraining, repractice, and retesting.

6. Follow-up
- Check employee job performance in following weeks to verify continuing competence.
- Monitor effectiveness of OJT program and competency of training.

Summary

1. There are both benefits and limitations to the use of self-study modules in training.

2. In preparing modules, all regular phases of planning for training need attention.

3. Special care should be given to selecting media for use in a module.

4. The study guide in a module consists of ten items.

5. In preparing to implement use of a module, plan for student orientation, instructor responsibilities, and maintaining student work records.

6. Gather reactions to at least twelve evaluation items when modules are used.

7. On-the-job training uses similar planning elements as with other training methods, including demonstration and supervision of the student.

Review Exercise

1. What three things, relating to the learning process, support the development and use of self-instructional modules?

2. Which items are *benefits* (B) and which are *limitations* (L) for self-instructional programs?
____ a. Each student may select topics and choose order for study.
____ b. Can relate to each student's training needs.
____ c. Every student may not favor this way to learn.
____ d. Some students may put off completion of study.
____ e. Some topics require frequent changes in training content.
____ f. Students set their own schedule for studying.

3. In what order should these components of a self-study module be presented in a study guide for student use?
____ a. Resources available for use.
____ b. Exercises and self-check tests.
____ c. Follow-up activities and applications.
____ d. Pretest for student.
____ e. Directions for using the module.
____ f. Study activities for each objective.
____ g. Learning objectives.
____ h. Remedial or review material to overcome lack of preparation.
____ i. Instructor evaluation.

4. To which aspect of implementing use of a self-study module (see page 151) does each action relate?
____ a. Take pretest.
____ b. Monitor progress.
____ c. Fulfill consultation role.
____ d. Record pretest results.
____ e. Learn how to operate resource equipment needed during study.
____ f. Note date student starts module.
____ g. Advise student how to proceed after pretest results are obtained.
____ h. Advise student when module completion is due.

5. Describe the difference between *structured* and *unstructured* methods of OJT.

6. Which statements are TRUE for successful OJT?
____ a. Specify learning objectives.
____ b. Teach knowledge rather than skill performance.
____ c. Avoid training when use of specialized equipment could disrupt normal operations.
____ d. Use checklists and rating scales to evaluate performance.
____ e. Allow student to study text or manual after seeing a demonstration before starting practice.
____ f. Only instructor talks as student watches and then carries out performance.
____ g. Assume successful OJT results will be applied on the job.
____ h. Develop job aids.

Answers: 1. Principles and conditions for learning.
Student preparation and learning styles.
Adult learning features.
2. Benefits – a,b,f; Limitations – c,d,e.
3. 1 – e; 2 – d; 3 – h; 4 – g; 5 – a; 6 – f; 7 – b; 8 – i; 9 – c.
4. Orientation – a,e,h; Instructor responsibility – b,c,g; Record results – d,f.
5. Structured OJT – developing and using a specific training plan with guarantee of learning.
Unstructured OJT – casual, haphazard learning as person picks up knowledge and skills from another employee.
6. a,c,d,h.

References

"A Basis for Instructional Alternatives." S. N. Postlethwait. *Journal of College Science Teaching, 21* (1981), 44-46.

"Design Strategies for Job Performance Aids." R. Smillie. In *Designing Usable Texts.* T. Duffy and R. Waller, eds. San Diego, CA: Academic Press, 1985.

Developing AV Instructional Modules for Vocational and Technical Training. N.T. Bell and A. J. Abedor. Englewood Cliffs, NJ: Educational Technology Publications, 1973.

"Guiding Performance with Job Aids." J. H. Harless. In *Introduction to Performance Technology,* volume 1. M. E. Smith, ed. Washington, DC: National Society for Performance and Instruction, 1986.

Improving Competency through Modular Instruction. J. D. Russell and K. A. Johanningemeier. Dubuque, IA: Kendall Hunt, 1981.

Individualizing Instruction: Making Learning Personal, Empowering and Successful. R. Hiemstra and B. Sisco. San Francisco: Jossey-Bass, 1990.

"Job Aids: Improving Employee Performance." G. Finnegan. *Performance and Instruction,* 1985, *24*(6), 10-11.

Learner-Controlled Instruction. F. Wydra. Englewood Cliffs, NJ: Educational Technology Publications, 1980.

"On-the-Job vs Classroom Training: Some Deciding Factors." S.L. Mangum. *Training,* 1985, *22*(2), 75-77.

"Supervisors as Trainers: The Long-Term Gain of OJT." S. B. Wehrenberg. *Personnel Journal,* 1987, *66*(4), 48-51.

Using Learning Contracts: Practice Approaches to Individualizing and Structuring Learning. M. Knowles. San Francisco: Jossey-Bass, 1986.

Chapter 17

HOW DO I CARRY-OUT CLASSROOM INSTRUCTION?

In this chapter you will learn to:

> • **Prepare the classroom for a training session.**
> • **Arrange for equipment use.**
> • **Develop your presentation skills.**
> • **Evaluate your presentation skills.**

Your planning for teaching a topic has been thorough and the time for the presentation is at hand. Visuals are ready, and printed material has been prepared. To ensure success in the classroom, the following details are helpful.

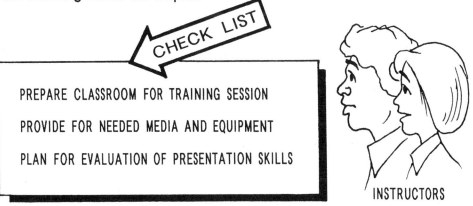

CHECK LIST

PREPARE CLASSROOM FOR TRAINING SESSION

PROVIDE FOR NEEDED MEDIA AND EQUIPMENT

PLAN FOR EVALUATION OF PRESENTATION SKILLS

INSTRUCTORS

Preparing the Room

In the classroom, tables, or chairs with a writing surface, may be permanently installed. But if they are movable, you may rearrange furniture to make the area a more informal work space, rather than only a formal, "sit-and-listen" room. If you want to encourage discussion, or have students work in small groups, then flexible arrangements must be planned for.

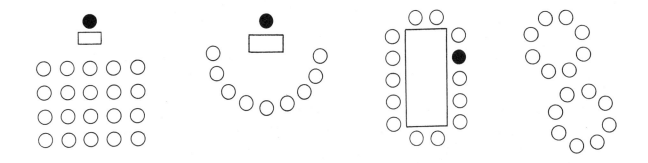

Also check room ventilation for good air circulation and the thermostat for a comfortable temperature.

Scheduling Equipment

The equipment specified in your lesson plan — projector, video player, items for demonstration — should be brought to the classroom. Check location of electrical outlets. Do not forget an extension power cord and an extra projection lamp.

Verify equipment operation. This includes setting size of projected image on the screen, focus, and sound level. Check seating for satisfactory viewing and comfort.

If a portable screen for projection will be used, decide on its best placement. You will want to restrict light from striking the screen so the image will be bright. Light entering from windows must be controlled. Room lights, located near the screen, should be turned off when projecting. Some light is necessary for note-taking and desirable for your eye contact with students. Adjust seating for satisfactory viewing.

Arrange materials for use. Refer to your lesson plan for when to distribute materials.

Presentation Skills

When you stand before a class of students and talk, show, or demonstrate, the success of your instruction relies on your presentation abilities. Even though the classroom setting is not a theatre stage, your professional bearing exhibited in front of the class is important. It helps with the impression you create and the cooperation you get from your students.

Do not write out a lecture and come to class prepared to read it. Use your lesson plan or make an outline along with notes. This can include examples, anecdotes, media use schedule and so forth.

For classroom instruction, the following points are important:

Appearance

The first impression that your students receive of you is a visual one — your appearance. An instructor who is neat and well groomed, will make a positive impression.

Speech

Speech is an instructor's chief communication tool. Use your voice in a natural, conversational way, but control it by varying the pitch and volume so your talking does not sound monotonous. Change the rate of speaking to give key points emphasis. Employ good diction and enunciate words clearly. Avoid expressions like "you know..." and "ah...ah..." before each thought.

Make sure your voice carries to the back of the room. If you are uncertain, ask students if they can hear you.

Use correct grammar. Do not ramble in your explanations. Develop a vocabulary about your subject that will help you to gain attention and hold interest. Write new words and unfamiliar expressions on the chalkboard.

Humor can make a point when you share a story or a situation from personal experience. Relating an incident or anecdote contributes to a positive rapport with students and gets them more involved mentally.

Use silence purposefully. Pause just before you state a key point and again when moving to the next segment of your presentation.

Mannerisms

Certain actions you exhibit can be distracting and disturbing to students. Avoid such things as finger pointing, fussing with a pencil or a piece of jewelry, jiggling coins in a pocket, adjusting clothing, pacing back and forth, or showing undesirable facial expressions like scowling.

You may not even be aware of such things. As will be suggested below, have someone videotape your presentation and then study the recording. You will quickly note any undesirable mannerisms that should be eliminated.

Asking Questions

The skill of questioning students during class is a valuable asset for an instructor. Proceed from general questions on a topic to more specific ones. Ask questions that are brief and easily understood. Allow a few seconds of silence before expecting a reply. This allows time for a person to organize a response. See page 45 for information on formulating various kinds of questions.

Some questions may be open to anyone for answering, while at other times, you may direct a question to a specific individual. Then allow other persons to confirm, amplify, or correct answers as necessary. Acknowledge good efforts.

Be Businesslike

Start the class period on time. Proceed with activities as outlined in your lesson plan and according to student expectations. End the class at the scheduled or agreed time.

Keep up with required recordkeeping. Attendance, grades, and other reports should be handled promptly and managed according to regulations.

Other Positive Behaviors

Learn the names of students in your class. Do this with a seating chart, or take individual pictures or a group photo. Then refer to each individual by name.

Be personally enthusiastic and dynamic in your actions and reactions. Use eye contact with individuals as you talk, and employ hand gestures in a natural way. Do not stand in one place all the time; move about occasionally. Handle your visual materials as an integral part of the lesson.

If you see a negative reaction or a perplexed look, do not ignore it. Pay attention to the body language students show. This may be leaning forward with anticipation or slumping back in their chairs. Do not put a student on the spot, and avoid making any sarcastic remarks or showing any favoritism to selected students.

Be approachable and sensitive to student needs. Exhibit patience and tolerance when a student's difficulties in understanding becomes evident.

Analysis and Improvement

If you are a recently assigned instructor, the above suggestions may not have real meaning until you are able to examine and analyze your own actions before a class. First of all, plan to rehearse your classroom presentations until you start to feel comfortable in front of students. You might also ask a colleague to observe both your rehearsals and a few classroom sessions, then to offer suggestions.

As noted above, it might be beneficial to arrange for a colleague to set up a video camcorder to document your presentation. If you would rather not do this during a regular class period, record the rehearsal in an empty classroom.

Place the camera where students would sit. Set the lens so your upper body will fill much of the frame. Thus, your actions will be clearly seen. Study the resulting tape. It will reveal your movements and expressions, both good and bad. Analyze the results, inviting reactions from colleagues, if you wish.

Practice to eliminate negative habits and improve on others. Sometime later, record another presentation and examine the results for improvement.

Carefully review the evaluations completed by students at the end of a previous course you conducted. (Hopefully, your organization has a policy of having students complete such an evaluation. See page 167 for an example.) Study comments and suggestions for your improvement.

Finally, there are many workshops and short courses on such topics as **Personal Presentation Skills** and **How to Speak Before a Group.** They are offered by colleges and commercial training companies. Also, in many areas of the country there are active chapters of Toastmasters, International. The organization's purpose is to help persons gain experience in making presentations before groups. Look into its services for your own benefits.

Summary

1. Prepare the classroom by arranging chairs and tables for the kinds of activities that will take place.

2. Place a portable screen for use so as to avoid direct light and adjust seating for satisfactory viewing.

3. Schedule, set-up and check equipment that will be used.

4. Do not read a prepared lecture; use an outline and notes.

5. Arrange materials for use and distribution to students.

6. Remember that your appearance, speech, and questioning techniques are all vital to your success as an instructor.

7. Analyze your classroom skills by having a colleague observe a rehearsal or a class presentation; record a lecture on videotape and evaluate it.

8. Review course evaluations by students for any benefits you may derive.

9. There are probably local workshops or short courses that can be taken to improve speaking and other presentation skills.

Review Exercise

1. Which of the following would be beneficial when carrying out training?
   ___ a. Show enthusiasm for your subject by tone of voice and physical movements.
   ___ b. Rarely use humor as it detracts from the seriousness of a class.
   ___ c. Start and end the class period promptly at assigned times.
   ___ d. Videotaping a classroom presentation is a good way to document your skills for analysis.
   ___ e. Judge your presentation skills for yourself without reference to evaluations by students.
   ___ f. The most important means a trainer has for communicating to students in class is through spoken words.
   ___ g. The first impression students receive of you is your physical appearance.
   ___ h. When explaining something, talk it all the way through with few pauses.
   ___ i. Set chairs in the classroom in formal, lined-up fashion for best control.
   ___ j. Keep scanning the class with your eyes rather than looking directly at individuals.
   ___ k. Avoid distracting movements like scowling or fussing with an object.
   ___ l. Place a projection screen where outside light will strike the surface for the brightest picture.
   ___ m. Expect an immediate reply to a question you ask or turn to another person for an answer.
   ___ n. Introduce new ideas with the jargon of your speciality so students will quickly learn new terms.

2. What two activities might you consider if you feel improving your classroom presentation skills becomes necessary?

Answers: 1. a,c,d,f,g,k.
        2. Ask a colleague to visit your class to observe your presentation.
          Have a class session videotaped.
          Attend a training seminar or workshop.

References

Delivering Effective Training. T. W. Goad. San Diego, CA: University Associates, 1982.

How To Be A Knockout With AV! Publication S-31. Rochester, NY: Eastman Kodak Company, 1990.

"Improving Instructor-Student Relationships." In *Instructing and Evaluating in Higher Education.* R.J. McBeath, ed. Englewood Cliffs, NJ: Educational Technology Publications, 1992.

Presenting Yourself. Publication S-60. Rochester, NY: Eastman Kodak Company, 1990.

Secrets of a Successful Trainer: A Simplified Guide tor Survival. C. Lambert. New York: Wiley and Sons, Publishers, 1986.

The Winning Trainer. J.E. Eitington. Houston, TX: Gulf Publishing, 1989.

Chapter 18

HOW DO I DETERMINE TRAINING RESULTS?

In this chapter you will learn to:

> • **Determine the effectiveness of your instruction.**
> • **Measure the efficiency of your instruction.**
> • **Calculate the costs of your training.**
> • **Design a questionnaire to gather student reactions.**
> • **Evaluate follow-up benefits of your training.**

Often an instructor is intuitively convinced that what happens in a training program is successful. The evidence to support such a conclusion may be limited. What is needed is unbiased, objective evidence that can help you to decide whether the need initially recognized (Chapter 1) has been satisfied.

By gathering necessary data, your intuition can be supported or rejected. You will have the facts for informing others in the department or organization about program results.

Furthermore, in the important legal climate that is widespread in our society, your liability for proper training and then certifying student competence would be protected if there is clear evidence of the success of your instruction. (See information on page xiv in the Introduction.) By keeping careful records, the procedures outlined in this chapter allow you to verify such success or direct you to improvements.

There are five important elements that allow you to judge the success of instruction:

- Effectiveness of a training program.
- Efficiency of a training program.
- Costs of a training program.
- Student and staff reactions to a training program.
- Follow-up benefits of a training program.

Immediately after a training program is concluded, some or all of the assessment methods to be described should be utilized. By following this procedure, trends and changes in program results can be tracked over time. Also, deficiencies can be noted as they show up, with corrections being made immediately.

Program Effectiveness

Effectiveness answers the question — **"To what degree did students accomplish the learning objectives prescribed for each topic of the course?"** Measurement of effectiveness can be determined from: test scores, performance, quality of products prepared, and other records that have been made of student learning results during the course.

An analysis of scores can be prepared by hand or through computer data-processing. From final results, a summary can be made to determine the degree to which students achieve the requirements specified by the learning objectives for a topic or the subject.

Here is an example of test results:

A. Topic Objectives	Test Questions for Objective
A	2,4,11
B	1,7
C	3,5,12
D	8,10
E	5,9

B. Student	Correct Answers to Questions (x)
	1 2 3 4 5 6 7 8 9 10 11 12
AJ	x x x x x x x x x x
SF	x x x x x x x x
TY	x x x x x x x x x x x
LM	x x x x x x x x x x x
RW	x x x x x x x x x x x
WB	x x x x x x x x x

C. Student	Objectives Satisfied
	A B C D E
AJ	x x x x
SF	x x x x
TY	x x x x x
LM	x x x x x
RW	x x x x x
WB	x x x x

In this example, the group of six students accomplished **90%** of the objectives. This figure is calculated by totaling the number of objectives satisfied — the **X** marks in Part C. The total is **27**. Divide by **6**, the number of students. The answer is **4.5**. This is the average number of objectives accomplished per trainee. It is **90%** of all five objectives. The percentage is a measure of the **effectiveness level** of the training program.

The instructor, often with organizational approval, should have previously decided the level at which to accept the program as being effective — **100%**, **90%**, or whatever. If the results do not indicate at least the acceptable level, then examine all components of the training (objectives, activities, test results, and so forth) to identify shortcomings. Make revisions for the next time the course is conducted.

Remember that the result of your instruction should be successful learning for as many students as possible. As considered on page 57, this **competency-based** method differs from the usual academic procedure of grading students on a normal curve with percentages representing their accomplishments (94%, 86%, 77% ...) or awarding letter grades (A-B-C...).

When we examine the effectiveness of a training program, we must recognize that there may be intangible outcomes (expressed as affective objectives) and long term consequences (like complex skills that can only be applied under realistic, on-the-job situations). Both of these items are treated in following sections. Here, the evaluation is limited to those learning objectives that can be measured during and at the end of the instructional program.

Program Efficiency

Efficiency answers the question "Was the course conducted with acceptable expenditures of **time, money,** and **effort?**"

Training programs are designed typically in terms of assigned time — one hour class session, three-hour period, five day sequence, school quarter or semester. If a conventional training program can be reduced from possibly a period of five days to four days, with the same or even increased effectiveness in learning, the program would be considered to be *more* efficient.

By carrying out the systematic planning as described in this book, contact time between instructor and students could be reduced. Thus, effort expended by a training staff becomes an important factor for greater efficiency and lower training costs. The balancing element could be increased self-study time by students in a learning center.

To reduce instructional time, such things as the following might be done:

- Revise activities and schedules.
- Increase use of media resources.
- Give students more responsibility for flexible, self-paced learning.

By changing from conventional, lock-step classroom training to a flexible, self-instructional method, you may find that both learning effectiveness and efficiency would be increased appreciably. While the development and preparation of instructional modules (Chapter 16) takes more time and requires greater initial support, the results, over a period of time, can be very positive.

Program Costs

In any organization, a major concern is the cost of training. This is the other factor affecting efficiency. The question to answer is — **"What does it cost to develop and then operate a specific program for the assigned number of students?"**

If an instructor, or a planning group, receives assigned time to develop the program, then **developmental** or "start-up" costs should be calculated. **Operational** costs are determined when the training takes place.

Developmental Costs
Translate as many of these items as would be feasible into actual costs:

- Planning time as portion of hourly or monthly salary for instructor or each member of planning group.
- Support time by secretary, other staff members, or consultants.
- Personnel time, supplies and materials for preparing materials, or cost for obtaining copies of print and media materials.
- Equipment obtained for this course.
- Other special services, office supplies, telephone, and travel costs.
- Indirect costs (portions of personnel benefits like health insurance and retirement) for time spent in planning.

> • Overhead (utilities, furniture depreciation, and other organizational services).

Operational Costs

Recurring operational costs each time the training takes place include as many of the following as applicable:

- Instructor's salary for time spent in training activities.
- Student costs, including salary received during training, travel, lodging, meals, or replacement cost for person filling in job.
- Time for any assistants, maintenance technicians, or others.
- Materials (handouts and consumables).
- Maintenance, repair of equipment, and replacement of damaged materials.
- Depreciation of equipment (portion of cost over anticipated lifetime).
- Overhead (utilities and furnishings).

Instructional Cost Index (cost per student)

Judging whether the cost of a training program is acceptable cannot be made by just adding up the amounts calculated for developmental and operational costs. Two additional factors must be considered:

- Actual number or anticipated average number of students in a class.
- Number of times the training program will be conducted before revision or termination would take place.

Use this procedure to calculate a final cost:

1. Decide for how many training periods the program will probably be used (For example every **two** weeks for a **four** month period total of **eight** times. This is the anticipated life of the program.)
2. Divide the developmental cost by the above number — **8**. This prorates the cost over the life of the program.
3. Add together the amount from #2 and the operational cost for one training period.
4. Determine the average number of students known or anticipated to be in the program with each use. Divide the total from #3 by this number. The result is the *cost per student*, or the **instructional cost index** for this course.

Here is an example of calculating an instructional cost index –

Total developmental cost	—	$ 1,000
Life of program	—	8 times
Portion of developmental cost	—	$ 122
Operational cost per use	—	$21,000
Number of students per use	—	30
INSTRUCTIONAL COST INDEX	—	$ 743

This index number has little meaning by itself. Compare it with other programs within a total training budget, or with comparable training programs in other organizations. By determining costs in this way, the instructor and administrators can have a basis on which comparisons can be made of the efficiency relating to the **cost benefits** for their training programs.

Subjective Measures

There are many other outcomes of training programs that should be examined during final evaluation. These include gathering reactions from both students and the training staff as they look back at the program just completed.

A **rating scale,** or **questionnaire,** can be developed and used to obtain information as to opinions about such things as:

- General value of the course.
- Level of usefulness of course content.
- Instructional methods used.
- Assistance received from instructor.
- Suggested course changes.

These opinion-gathering tools are similar to the instruments used to determine student attitude and expectations at the start of a training program. (See page 33.) If you obtained opinions at that time, you may want to compare them with those gathered now.

Here are examples of subjective evaluations:

(A). **Course Rating scale:**

To what extent do you agree or disagree with each statement? Circle the proper number.

	Strongly agree				Strongly disagree
1. Course is well organized.	1	2	3	4	5
2. Course topics were relevant.	1	2	3	4	5
3. Instructor presentations were valuable.	1	2	3	4	5
4. Class time seemed to drag.	1	2	3	4	5
5. Handouts were useful.	1	2	3	4	5
6. Visuals helped me to learn.	1	2	3	4	5
7. Practical activities helped to clarify content.	1	2	3	4	5
8. I felt free to ask questions.	1	2	3	4	5
9. Working with others helped my learning.	1	2	3	4	5
10. Testing was fair.	1	2	3	4	5

Are there changes you would suggest in this course?

(B). Instructor Rating by Student:

	Low				High
1. Made subject interesting and understandable.	1	2	3	4	5
2. Showed enthusiasm for subject .	1	2	3	4	5
3. Made good use of examples and visuals.	1	2	3	4	5
4. Was helpful coach during practice sessions.	1	2	3	4	5
5. Used class time effectively.	1	2	3	4	5
6. Provided useful information as feedback.	1	2	3	4	5
7. Shows respect for students.	1	2	3	4	5
8. Encourages student participation during class.	1	2	3	4	5

(C). Questionnaire:

The following questions apply to the course you have just completed. Answer each question briefly.

1. Did you find the course of value to your job responsibilities?

2. Which topics were most relevant to your needs?

3. Did you receive sufficient attention from the instructor when working on your project?

4. Did you find the self-paced activities a useful way to learn?

5. Was your learning fairly evaluated?

Follow-up Benefits

The major reason for a technical training program is to initiate, improve, upgrade, or extend competencies in a specific subject or aspect of a job. Recall that in Chapter 1 we stated that training should be used to serve identified needs. The goal for any program should be derived from such needs. Therefore, now it is important to obtain answers to this question — **"After completing training, how well do individuals perform in their work (quality of products, services performed, attitudes, etc.), in terms of the goal for the training program and specific objectives for topics?"**

This question, transposed into a questionnaire or other information-gathering form, can be used with supervisors, former students, and co-workers. The evaluation can be made periodically after training. The results may indicate that the benefits of training continue to be satisfactory, or there may become a need for further training.

Follow-up Questionnaire:

The purpose of the training program that _____
completed was to _____.
(learn a new skill, increase productivity, improve safety,
and so forth).

1. What changes in performance do you now find?

2. Are these what you expected?

3. Has the program had an effect on the _____
   (operation, productivity, safety, etc.) of your department?

4. Should other employees take this training?

5. How do you feel about the amount of time required for
   this training?

Training Program Modification and Improvement

When you examine the training results for each of the categories treated in this chapter, ask yourself these questions:

- In terms of learning objectives for the subject, is student learning at an acceptable level? **(effectiveness)**
- Are time periods assigned or available for classroom training, group activities, and self-paced learning, of sufficient length, or might the training period be shortened? **(efficiency)**
- At the conclusion of the course, are student attitudes and opinions expressed positively? **(affective evaluation)**
- Are the individuals competent on the job as the result of training? **(follow-up)**

If your answer to any of these questions is not fully acceptable, determine where modification in the program would be necessary. Consider these questions:

- Were learning objectives appropriate to the topic and properly understood by students?
- Were students suitably prepared for the training?
- Were classroom, group, and individual activities appropriate to accomplish specific objectives?
- Did the media and other resources contribute satisfactorily to learning?
- Did testing methods and individual questions properly measure accomplishment of specific objectives?
- Was the instructor knowledgeable in the content and competent in teaching?

Based on answers to these last questions, evaluate the lesson plans developed and used for each topic. Examine all course materials. Identify components that need revision and improvement before the training would be conducted again.   Repeat this evaluation at the completion of each training course.

Another reason for modifying training may be changes in on-the-job operating procedures and new equipment-use requirements. Gathering responses periodically by using the Follow-up Benefits category of training results can reveal these needs and the actions you could take for improvement.

Summary

1. Effectiveness is a measure of the degree to which students accomplish a topic's learning objectives. Ideal effectiveness would be ALL students accomplishing ALL objectives at the required performance level.

2. Efficiency considers the time, money, and effort required in a training program. The less staff time devoted to the course (with satisfactory effectiveness) the better the efficiency.

3. Training program costs include both developmental and operational costs: the former prorated and the latter for each time the class or course is conducted.

4. An instructional cost index can be calculated as the cost per student, and is useful for comparing cost benefits of training programs.

5. Subjective evaluations by students to a training program can be gathered by using a rating scale or a questionnaire.

6. There are benefits to determining how well students perform on the job after completing a training program. Use a rating scale or questionnaire to gather data.

7. On the bases of all program evaluation methods, determine where program modification and improvement may be necessary.

Review Exercise

1. To which training program results does each statement relate?
____ a. Length of time for conducting a course
____ b. Planning and instructional times
____ c. Questionnaire on opinions
____ d. Results of test scores and skill ratings
____ e. Level of trainee accomplishment of objectives
____ f. Program costs

2. What is the *effectiveness* of instruction for this group of students?
Student: A B C D E F G H
Objectives satisfied: 7 9 6 8 8 9 7 10
    (total = 10)

3. Determine an instructional cost index from the following:

Developmental cost   — $5,000
Operational cost   — $2,500
Anticipated times to have course   —   5
Number of students in class   —   20
Instructional cost index $_____

4. What are three questions that you would want to ask to determine the value of a training program after its completion?

5. What items should be identified if a training program is shown to need improvement?

Answers: 1. a – efficiency, b – program costs, c – subjective measures, d – effectiveness, c – effectiveness, f – efficiency.
         2. 80% effective.
         3. Instructional cost index — $175.
         4. Is student learning at an acceptable level?
           Is the training time of sufficient length or can it be shortened?
           Are student reactions positive to the program?
           Are students competent at work after training?
         5. Learning objectives.   Media uses.
           Student preparation.   Testing learning.
           Instructional activities.

References

"Analyzing the Costs and Benefits of Training." G. Kearsley. *Performance and Instruction,* 1987, *25*(1), 30-32; (3), 23-25; (4), 13-16; (5), 8-10; (6) 8-9.

Costs, Benefits and Productivity in Training Systems. G. Kearsley. Reading, MA: Addison-Wesley, 1982.

"Developing Opinion, Interest, and Attitude Questionnaires." In *Instructing and Evaluating in Higher Education*. R. J. McBeath, ed. Englewood Cliffs, NJ: Educational Technology Publications, 1992.

Designing Effective Instruction and Learning. Chapter 18. J. E. Kemp, G. R. Morrison, and S. M. Ross. Columbus, OH: Macmillan, 1993.

"Evaluating Training Programs in Business and Industry." In *New Directions for Program Evaluation*, no. 44. R. E. Brinkerhoff, ed. San Francisco: Jossey-Bass, 1989.

How to Measure Training Effectiveness. L. Rae. New York: Nichols, 1986.

"Measuring the *Goodness* of Training." J. Gordon. *Training*, 1991, *28*(8), 19-25.

More Evaluating of Training Programs. D. Kirkpatrick, ed. Alexandria, VA: American Society for Training and Development, 1988.

"Training: What's It Worth?" J. Cullen and others. *Training and Development Journal,* 1976, *30*(8), 12-20.

Training Cost Analysis: A Practical Guide. G. Head. Washington, DC: Marlin Press, 1985.

Epilogue

After studying the chapters of this book, you should be aware that preparation to conduct technical training is a mental activity that requires examining a number of essential components.

Many chapter headings were stated in the form of a question because, as you go through the phases of planning, you need to ask yourself those types of questions. They can alert you to what you need to do to focus your efforts on the specifics.

After you carry out the procedures a few times, you should feel comfortable with the process. Recognize that you can modify any planning components and rearrange the order of their application as you prefer.

We hope you have been motivated to try some of the new approaches to training described in this book. By supplementing or replacing a lecture with a form of self-paced learning, you can provide a more flexible means for training. Then, you will find your role as a facilitator and manager of learning more productive.

You may now find it advantageous to return to the Questionnaire near the front of the book (page xvii). Rate yourself again as you now anticipate applying these planning procedures. This final activity can serve as a good review of the total process. If you do this, you can better understand previously unfamiliar items and now recognize their value for training.

Training can be a useful, enjoyable experience that provides satisfaction to both instructor and students.

Good luck in developing your plans for training and then in carrying out the planning ... with success!

Glossary

affective domain   includes learning for attitudes, personal feelings, and interpersonal relations

authoring system   computer software which takes a program developer step-by-step through the development of a computer-based training program

back light   separates the person or object in a scene from the background

barcode reader   a penlike unit that can scan patterns of printed vertical lines, sending a signal for precisely accessing frames on videotape or a videodisc branching format program structured with optional paths so a student might choose or be directed to follow a certain arrangement of program elements

CAI   *see* computer-based training

CBT   *see* computer-based training

CD   *see* compact disc

CD-I   compact disc interactive; uses CD-ROM discs and can respond to computer commands

CD-ROM   compact disc read only memory; stores large amounts of information as text, graphics, pictures, and sound

camcorder   combines videocamera and tape recorder into a single unit

checklist   an evaluation instrument containing list of sequential steps or other actions that can be marked off as a student performs the skill

clip art   collections of commercially-prepared art in booklets or computer graphics software

closeup shot   a close view of specific details of a subject within a scene

cognitive domain   factual information and thought processes relative to a topic

compact disc   4 3/4 inch disc on which sound, data, and visuals may be recorded and read with a laser beam

competency-based training   training that can be evaluated against a specific standard as indicated by the learning objectives for a topic or skill

computer-assisted instruction   see computer-based training

computer-based training   using a personal computer for studying a topic with appropriate software that consists of text, graphics, and possibly other visuals for interactive learning

computer projector panel   a device for direct projection of computer-generated data on an overhead projector

concept   name or expression given to a class of facts, objects, or events, all of which have common features

conditions   part of a learning objective that describes any circumstance under which the required learning is to take place

continuity   the logical relationship as one scene leads to the next one with smooth flow of action

criterion-referenced instruction   a training program based on a specific set of learning objectives having a direct relationship with test items for evaluating learning

DVI   digital video interactive; uses CD-ROM discs to store up to 72 minutes of motion video and audio information as compressed, digital signals

deductive method   moving from an overview of a topic to details for each part

desktop publishing   preparation of printed materials using a personal computer with a word processing program, graphics software, and a high-resolution printer

developmental costs   all personnel, resources, and services costs required to plan and develop a training program

documentary   videorecording activities as they normally take place, without following a detailed script

effectiveness of training   measuring the degree to which students accomplish objectives specified for a topic or total course

efficiency of training   measuring the time, money, and effort required to carry-out a training program and then deciding if the amounts are acceptable or excessive

electronic still camera   records images on 2-inch disk that are viewed on a computer screen or on a TV receiver via a photo CD player

essay test   questions that require a student to write an answer that organizes and expresses thoughts in a logical way

establishing shot   view that establishes the location of a subject

feedback   providing the student with answers to questions and the level of performance as progress in learning

fill light   softens or eliminates shadows produced by the key light

flowchart   visual description of the sequence necessary for performing a task, including decision points and alternate paths

goal broad statement describing what should take place in an instructional course or training program

hard skills relate to psychomotor or physical skill learning

high angle shot scene recorded with the camera placed high, looking down at the subject

HyperMedia linking textual material and multimedia forms that can be viewed in any preferable arrangement (*see* also HyperText)

HyperText software programs that allow user to retrieve information by navigating from one element of content to another by using icons or other search strategies

inductive approach moving from an examination of each part of a topic to an overview or understanding of the complete subject

instructional cost index calculation of the cost per student to accomplish objectives for a topic or a course, taking into account a portion of the developmental cost and full operational cost

instructional objectives *see* learning objectives

interactive computer/video presentation of video images in a preferred sequence as controlled by a computer program or by student choice

interactive learning interplay between a person and media wherein the student controls the pace and often the sequence for learning

job aid learning tool in the form of a description, a checklist of steps, or illustration of procedures for individual use when learning or reviewing information to perform a skill

key light main source of light for a scene

learning objective statement containing up to four parts that describe what the student is specifically required to learn or accomplish relative to a topic or a skill

learning styles various methods of learning as preferred by individuals or which may be more effective with different individuals

linear format program structured in a set order so a student moves sequentially through the program

long shot general view of a subject and its setting

low angle shot scene recorded with the camera placed low, looking up at the subject

mastery learning provides quality instruction with necessary study time and active learning opportunities for a student to accomplish the specific objectives for a topic or subject

medium shot view of a subject that eliminates unnecessary background and other details

mock-up a simplified model of a real object

model recreation of a real object that may be smaller or larger than the original

module *see* self-study module

multiple choice test questions consisting of a stem with a number of options or alternatives from which a students selects an answer

needs analysis study of performance and other factors that affect job effectiveness with recommendations for improvement

normal curve illustrates traditional method of distributing students' relative accomplishment within a class and leading to assignment of A-B-C-D-F grades

OJT *see* on-the-job training

objective *see* learning objective

objective-type tests questions for which a student must select an answer from two or more alternatives, including multiple choice and true/false forms

on-the-job training direct training for one individual or a few employees in the actual work environment with equipment used on the job

operational costs all personnel, resources, and services costs incurred when a training program is implemented

overhead transparency information prepared on 8 1/2"x11" plain or treated acetate sheets for use on a projector placed at the front of a classroom

pan (panorama) shot the movement of a videocamera while shooting in a horizontal plane (left and right)

performance level part of a learning objective that describes the standard under which the required learning is to take place

platform teaching lecture method as instructor presents information to students

prerequisite knowledge or skill background or preparation a student has for studying a subject

pretest test given students prior to start of instruction to determine level of preparation relative to a topic or skill

principle high level generalization derived from a set of concepts

psychomotor domain physical action or skill involving muscles of the body

rating scale evaluation instrument consisting of a numerical scale with descriptive criteria that can be marked to judge quality and quantity of a resulting product or student achievement

reinforcement providing the student with feedback on success in learning, thus being encouraged to continue learning

rule *see* principle

scene description of a subject for each element in a script

script specific directions for picture-taking and accompanying sound in the form of a list of scenes with narration, other sounds, or captions

self-paced learning allowing students to accomplish required learning through activities at one's own speed and convenience

self-study module package for individual student to study a topic that consists of a detailed study guide and accompanying media materials

sequence number of related shots put together to show a single event, relating to a subject

short answer test questions that require a student to answer with a single word, phrase, sentence, or numbers

shot action in a video scene recorded each time the start button is activated and then released

simulation representation of a real-life problem or situation, often presented in a media form, for a student or a group to solve or react to

soft skills relate to affective learning treating attitudes, personal feelings, and interpersonal relations

still video camera *see* electronic still camera

storyboard series of sketches or pictures that visualize each sequence in an instructional material

structured OJT carefully designed plan for on-the-job training

synchronized sound sounds on audiotape or videotape that correlate in proper relationship with pictures

tilt shot movement of a videocamera in a vertical plane (up and down)

true/false test questions as statements for which a student must decide if each is true or false, or otherwise Yes or No.

unstructured OJT casual way that on-the-job training can be conducted as one person assists another to learn

video projection stand device that looks like an overhead projector, consists of a small video camera that can transmit images of slides, transparencies, pictures, diagrams, and real objects for viewing on a TV receiver

videodisc most commonly 12" disc containing 54,000 still image frames, 30 minutes of motion, or a combination of the two

zoom shot with use of a special lens, scene appears to move closer or away from the camcorder

INDEX

Index